WARNING:

LIVING IS DANGEROUS TO YOUR HEALTH

By

Glenda C. Finkelstein

Final Destiny Press
Plant City Florida 33565

Cover Photo: Veda Gonzalez | Dreamstime.com
Cover Design: Tony E. Finkelstein
Edited By: Dr. Tammy L. Ferrante

Library of Congress Control Number: 2015910375
Final Destiny Press, Plant City Fl.

1st Edition Published, 1999 By Author House
(1st Books Library) ISBN: 0-7596-8370-0
2nd Edition Published, 2015 By Final Destiny Press,
ISBN: 978-0-9914090-1-3

Dedicated to the Glory of God, and to the Empowerment of His children.

A special thanks to Reverend and Mrs. Deon Lett
And Pastor Ed and Janis Russo

Table of Contents

Chapter One

_____In the beginning, there was the alarm clock.... 9

Chapter Two

_____Road Warriors and Speed Demons................................. 19

Chapter Three

_____The good, the rude, and the indifferent............................. 29

Chapter Four

_____Fat Phantom vs. Heavenly Manna.. 41

Chapter Five

_____Mistakes, Errors, and Oops. Oh my!.................................. 51

Chapter Six

_____Traffic Jams 63

Chapter Seven

_____Stress Giant Defeated!... 75

Chapter Eight

_____To sin, or not to sin?... 89

Chapter Nine

_____Be Happy! 99

Chapter Ten

_____Keep the Sabbath!.. 109

Chapter Eleven

_____Now I lay me down to sleep.. 127

<u>Chapter One</u>

In the beginning, there was the alarm clock....

Somewhere in the wee hours of the morning before the sun breaks the horizon, your alarm clock buzzes creating an unholy sound that disturbs your peaceful slumber. This sudden noise yanks you away from the best dream you've had all night as your body retches toward the nightstand to slap that infernal contraption that so rudely catapulted you into consciousness. Whether your alarm clock buzzes, rings or plays music it is the most dread sound any human confronts second only to nails on a chalkboard. You can achieve five more minutes of slumber, but it too will shatter when the alarm reminds you it's still time to get up. Again, you take just five more minutes. When you finally decide to get up now or face the consequences of running late, you turn to the alarm clock perhaps with a not so pleasant comment on your lips, turn it off, and get up. Does this sound familiar?

Why is it that we put ourselves through this torture? If we couldn't stand the sound the first time, why do we believe that five more minutes will allow us the pleasure of sleep without having to get out of bed? Why should we dread the morning preferring the fantasy of our dreams or just the oblivion of not having to consciously face the day? It's the beginning of a new day. It's a chance to improve upon our yesterday on an unwritten page in our lives chock full of possibilities. For some reason we take a more pessimistic approach especially if it's a work day.

Each person is different in how they greet the morning. In my home for instance, we are split down the middle with half of us considered morning people and the other half non-morning people. My son is not considered a morning person. His body must thaw ever so slowly from the ice age of sleep. If it proceeds too quickly, he gets angry demanding the world around him to leave him alone. On the other hand, my daughter is a morning person. She awakens immediately and believes everyone in the house should partake in her joyous good fortune. She gives perky a whole new meaning.

Usually, what we dread is not the rising of the sun, but being stuck in the mindset that this day will be just the same as yesterday with no improvement. Be it work, school, chores, or dealing with difficult situations we do not look upon a new day as a blessing. After all, we have no trouble getting up for vacation, but it takes a near miracle to get to work on time. Ready or not, however, it's time to face the world and pick up where we left off the day before. The child of God, however, will not be facing this new day alone.

Lamentations 3:21-23
This I recall to my mind, therefore I have hope. Through the Lord's mercies we are not consumed, because His compassions fail not. They are new every morning; Great is Your faithfulness. - NKJV

Now that we know that the mercies of the Lord are with us fresh each day without fail, we have no reason to dread the coming day. As encouraging as these words of truth are, we still struggle with our day don't we? Perhaps it is because we have not properly prepared ourselves. Think about it. You wouldn't dream about going to school or work without bringing your supplies, eating breakfast, or being properly dressed, etc. The same is true about walking in faith and making yourself different from the world. This should be a joyous task and not drudgery, but what should we do first?

Luke 22:46
Then He said to them, "Why do you sleep? Rise and pray, lest you enter into temptation." –NKJV

The above scripture is a command by Christ, to His disciples in the garden of Gethsemane, who had fallen asleep to get up and pray so that they wouldn't fall into temptation during difficult times. In many ways, the children of God have fallen asleep, and we need prayer to keep us from the temptations of the world. Prayer, although powerful, is not the whole of our obedience to God.

Ephesians 6:13-18
Therefore, take up the full armor of God, that you may be able to resist in the evil day, and having done everything, to stand firm. Stand firm therefore, having girded your loins with truth, and having put on the breastplate of righteousness, and having shod your feet with the preparation of the gospel of peace; in addition to all, taking up the shield of faith with which you will be able to extinguish all the flaming missiles of the evil one. And take up the helmet of salvation, and the sword of the Spirit, which is the word of God. With all prayer and petition pray at all times in the Spirit, and with this in view, be on the alert with all perseverance and petition for all the saints. –NASB

This is quite a directive, and so necessary. To sum it up in just a few words, spend some quality time with God. Spending time in the presence of God is more important than spending quality time with your spouse, child, sibling, friend, or parent. By seeking God, first we will by association, become a better parent, spouse, or child. He teaches us to be accepting, forgiving, and patient with each other and ourselves.

You say that your schedule it too busy. If the enemy has his way, you will always be too busy. Make the time. Here are two examples between being prepared and not being prepared. The first is a morning that you didn't spend time with God.

Morning without spending time with God

The alarm rings and you slap it a few times. You make your way slowly to the shower, turn on the water, and let it fall upon you. After that, you shuffle to the pot of coffee waiting in the kitchen. It's empty. Great, you have to make the coffee, but where is it?

"Mommy, mommy, I can't find my socks," child number one calls out in frustration.

"Mom, where are my shoes?" Child number two asks.

"Honey, where is my briefcase?" Spouse questions in his usual hurry.

"Daddy! Sister is flicking milk at me," child number two says in complaint.

"Stop kicking me! Daddy brother is kicking me!" Child number one screams.

"Stop fighting! Eat your breakfast!" Dad bellows.

"Where did you put the coffee?" You ask.

"I don't know, I put it where it always goes," spouse answers.

"Mommy, daddy sprinkled coffee on my cereal!" Child number one complains.

Having heard enough of this chaos, you come out of the kitchen and make a totally ludicrous statement: "If you don't stop fighting and yelling, I'm going to throw all of you to the moon!" (I could go on, but you get the general idea.)

Morning after spending time with God

13

Glenda C. Finkelstein

You awake before the alarm sounds. You shower, pray, and read the Bible. After that, you shuffle to the pot of coffee waiting in the kitchen. It's empty. Great, you have to make the coffee, but where is it?

"Mommy, mommy, I can't find my socks," child number one complains.

"Mom! Where are my shoes?" Child number two asks.

"Honey, where is my briefcase?" Spouse questions in his usual hurry.

"Daddy! Sister is flicking milk at me!"

"Stop kicking me! Daddy brother is kicking me!" Child number one complains.

"Stop fighting! Eat your breakfast!" Dad bellows.

"Where did you put the coffee?" You ask.

"I don't know, I put it where it always goes," Spouse answers.

"Mommy, daddy sprinkled coffee on my cereal!" Child number one complains.

Having heard enough of this chaos, you come out of the kitchen and start to make a totally ludicrous statement, but wait, this sounds all too familiar. What happened to the strength of our Lord, and the shield? Nothing, it is still there, but it is within us, not within our circumstances. Faith does not come in trial size. You probably had to fight to stay awake while you read the Bible and prayed, and you feel defeated saying nothing has changed.

14

Faith is not some instant mix that you can pour out of a box. There are no shortcuts to faith. Faith comes one step at a time, but to add to your faith you must have a foundation to build upon. That foundation is the Word of God, the mortar is praise, and the support beams are prayer. Each trial and experience, when met with these three, will add a stone of faith. Faith is not without cost. You must earn it by your toil. Should you stumble, however, He is still faithful.

2 Timothy 2:11-13
It is a trustworthy statement. For if we died with Him, we shall also live with Him; If we endure, we shall also reign with Him; If we deny Him, He also will deny us; If we are faithless, He remains faithful; for He cannot deny Himself. –NASB

You may not even notice the small change made on that first day that you prayed and read the word, but do it again and again and again. Before long you will notice that you are not only different, but the people around you will start to notice this difference too. You will discover that the minor disruptions of the morning will not dictate the rest of your day. Who cares if you have on two different colors of socks that you don't notice until you get to the office? If a rock star did it, they would be setting a new fashion trend. Be bold, laugh at yourself. Life is serious enough without letting the smallest of things bring us down into the mud.

Glenda C. Finkelstein

Am I saying that you will never lose your temper? No, as we are all very human and must learn to master our emotions and forgive ourselves when we mess up. As a mother of two children they are the source of my greatest joy, and the two of them can cause my emotions to change from happy to infuriated, in zero point seven seconds. Just like you I am learning. I don't have all the answers, but am seeking the Lord, who does for guidance. In my journey, I have also discovered that the more time I spend with God, the less I want to be away from Him and my family is following in my example. I'm not saying to keep your head so much in heavenly things that you are no earthly good. We have a lot of work to do here, and it is what we do outside the church that is being studied. In that light, we should always be mindful to be a good testimony.

Colossians 3:17
And whatever you do in word or deed, do all in the name of the Lord Jesus, giving thanks through Him to God the Father. – NASB

I strive daily to live this scripture in every aspect of my life. I work for my employer as if I were serving the Lord. God recognizes that, and my employer has blessed me for it because of God's favor. Even if my employer didn't notice, I would still do the same because God notices. Even enduring trials I have noticed that I have gained blessings from God that I didn't even know I gained until I saw through the eyes of others. Patience is a good
16

example. I have never considered myself to be a patient person. Many times I would vent to my friends at work about my children. They make comments like, "You have such patience. We could never deal with that as calmly as you did." At first I look at them as if they are crazy, but when I think about how I deal with stress now as opposed to a few years ago. I realize I have grown in patience.

While going through daily stresses and problems, we become so blind that we don't see how this could make us stronger. We also tend to believe that the only real reward to going through these times is getting to the end of them. There is so much to gain from these trials, but we often miss the mark and become swept up in them instead of overtaking them.

James 1:12
Blessed is a man who perseveres under trial; for once he has been approved, he will receive the crown of life, which the Lord has promised to those who love Him. –NASB

Don't let your circumstances deceive you into thinking that your daily devotions are useless. Remain in the word and stay in prayer no matter how much the temperature may rise. Use every morning as a new beginning knowing that your comments and your actions may make the difference in eternity for someone watching your life. You may not feel as if you have much faith, but to someone else your faith may seem to be like a fortress. Where you go, others will follow toward life or destruction. The time is short and the days are evil. Never before has there been such a need to really know the Lord. We need to stop playing church and make our relationship with God our first priority. Being too busy will not hold any water on judgment day. Trust God because He knows what we need, it was He who made a time for everything. All we have to do is make sure we keep our priorities in order.

Matthew 6:33
But seek first His kingdom and His righteousness; and all these things shall be added to you. – NASB

<u>Chapter Two</u>

Road Warriors and Speed Demons

It may be that not everyone's morning starts out like the one in the previous chapter. Perhaps it's not until we drive to school or work that the real stress begins. I mean which of us has not had the experience of driving by the rules and laws of the road, just to have someone speed around us as if we were a tortoise. Every time that happens to me it brings back memories of the child who thought he or she was so special that they could skip to the front of the lunchroom line. I mean really, just who do they think they are? Don't act so spiritual, you know you really get a kick out of it when the car that just passed you going eighty miles an hour gets stuck at the same traffic light you do.

Then there is the tailgater. Just once, we want that police officer to see the jerk who was following you so close that if you sneezed he would become a permanent part of your trunk. Perhaps it's not the one who is speeding that makes you so exasperated, but the one who just jumped out in front of you going five miles per hour. These people drive as if demon possessed, but what is worse

19

we find ourselves acting just like them. You know the person tailgating you just wants to pass you, but you want to make them earn it so you speed up or keep pace with another car so they can't pass. All this behavior does is increase their anger. Many times we place ourselves at great risk, and what are we fighting over any way. It's usually one car length of pavement. Is that small piece of road worth losing your life? I believe all of us would answer with a resounding NO on that point, but is it worth losing your witness? That's a little different. How can we lose our witness by getting upset? After all, we are still human and subject to the flesh in which we live out our lives on earth. My boss always says that the true test of how much control we have is found only when it's tested by stress.

Proverbs 15:1
A soft answer turns away wrath, but a harsh word stirs up anger. –NKJV

Road rage comes in many forms, and much of the situation could be diffused if we chose a softer response. The most violent cases have killed innocent people for nothing more than to get one car length ahead of them. Most of us, however, wind up losing our temper and by the time we reach our destination we are grumpy and downright contemptible. This loss of self-control starts us down a path of grumbling and complaining which leads to more angry words and actions. Not a very good testimony is it? All of us have been guilty of this at one time or another.

Man's anger brings death as so many news reports have informed us. How many people die every single day because of man's rage and loss of self-control? When we get behind the wheel of a car, we are taking control of an object that can kill. We seem to forget that thinking that cars are merely a means of transportation, but in reality they are the most attainable weapon that we have at our disposal. It kills because the operator made a mistake, got angry, had no self-control, became ill, or merely became distracted. I realize that there have been some very tragic losses of life where innocent people died through no fault of their own. There is a cause for each accident. Webster's New World Dictionary defines the word *Accident: as a happening that is not expected, foreseen, or intended.*

How many times have we said something in anger that if we had been in control, would have never left our lips? I submit to you that anger is the immediate fleshly response to a situation that offended our flesh. Take our desire to be first in line. If you have more than one child or siblings, you can relate to this first hand. No one likes to be at the end of the line. The world speaks it out loud and clear in every aspect of our lives. Self, number one, and be a winner. Just the fact of being the first person in a line of many, however, does not grant you authority or leadership. It is nothing more than the place you happen to be standing. If you changed the perspective of the line, the one who seemed to be last is now at the head. Now let's take a look at anger of the flesh as viewed by the spirit.

James 1:19-22
This you know, my beloved brethren. But let everyone be quick to hear, slow to speak, and slow to anger; for the <u>anger of man does not achieve the righteousness of God</u>. Therefore putting aside all filthiness and all that remains of wickedness, in humility receive the word implanted, which is able to save your souls. But prove yourselves doers of the word, and not merely hearers who delude themselves. – NASB

James is pretty clear that we must act on the word of God not just listen to it. Otherwise, we are no different from a non-believer. The old adage of taking a deep breath and count to ten before reacting to a situation that made you angry is quite practical. By waiting before we respond we have a chance to ascertain the other individual's true reason for being angry. Angry words or a heated tone spoken at a given situation could find their venting outlet hurled on you, instead of what really made them angry. You become the lucky recipient of their frustration. Instead of feeling punished as a victim, turn it into an opportunity to minister. Is it easy? No, it takes a great deal of self-control, discernment, and wisdom.

Proverbs 22:24-25

Do not associate with a man given to anger; or go with a hot-tempered man, lest you learn his ways and find a snare for yourself. –NASB

Human nature often finds us imitating those around us. Solomon understood this and chose to share this wisdom. Unfortunately later in his reign he did not follow his own advice making bad choices in marriage that ultimately led him away from God. If Solomon, the wisest man that ever lived, can fall so can we. Although we have the commission to be witnesses to the ends of the earth, we are to be separate. We must minister Christ's love to the world, but our fellowship is with the body of Christ.

Proverbs 14:29
He who is slow to anger has great understanding, but he who is quick-tempered exalts folly. –NASB

I once witnessed two men after they had a minor fender bender on the road begin fighting with one another instead of remaining calm and contacting the authorities to complete the proper paperwork. When the light changed, they stopped, jumped into their vehicles and raced down the crowded street a few blocks away just to get out and continue fighting again at the next red light. The damage done to either vehicle was very minor, but their actions placed many people including children in great danger because it blinded them to reason. Luckily the rest of us survived their folly.

Glenda C. Finkelstein

Genesis 49:7
Cursed be their anger, for it is fierce; and their wrath for it is cruel. I will disperse them in Jacob, and scatter them in Israel. –NASB

In Genesis, Jacob curses his sons Simeon and Levi for their vicious cruelty. They lacked mercy and compassion. They allowed anger to rule their minds. They acted without thinking. You probably agree with Jacob. After all, they lamed animals and killed people. Jacob, however, did not curse them for killing or laming. He cursed them for their anger. We may not have killed anyone with a sword, but how many people have we wounded with an angry word?

James 3:10
Out of the same mouth proceed blessing and cursing. My brethren, these things ought not to be. –NKJV

Now that we have a feel for what anger is and where it leads us all too quickly. Let's find some ways we can keep it under submission to the spirit of God that resides in every Christian.

Proverbs 12:18
There is one who speaks rashly like the thrusts of a sword, but the tongue of the wise brings healing. –NASB

24

By being slow to speak, we can stop the sharp words and make them words of reconciliation. We can express our differences in kindness instead of disregard. It's not easy especially in heated moments, but it's not impossible. The Holy Spirit will give us that strength if we ask.

Psalm 34:13-14
Keep your tongue from evil, and your lips from speaking deceit. Depart from evil, and do good; seek peace and pursue it. –NASB

In other words, mind your own business. Don't spread gossip or unkind words about another. As most mothers' are so fond of saying, "If you can't say something nice, don't say anything at all." I make it a habit to speak only those things that would not bring harm to another. I once walked into a conversation about myself. The other two women had no idea I was standing there. The story being spun was so interesting and very surprising, but not as surprising as the look on their faces when I sat down at their table and asked them to continue. I told them I had no idea I had such an exciting adventure and then offered them the truth. Needless to say, they were very pale and speechless for a while. The truth was of interest to them, and I told them the next time they heard such a story to come ask me. Remember the person you may be discussing may not be there, but God is.

Glenda C. Finkelstein

Proverbs 15:2-4
The tongue of the wise makes knowledge acceptable, but the mouth of fools spouts folly. <u>The eyes of the Lord are in every place, watching the evil and the good.</u> A soothing tongue is a tree of life, but perversion in it <u>crushes the spirit.</u> — NASB

When faced with someone that is rude or obnoxious, don't be like a fool and follow in their ways. Let them have their piece of pavement or their say. Don't return anger for anger. As anger fuels, anger, kind words or a calm spirit will squelch anger's fire. You may not ever see that person again, but returning kindness for rudeness received may make a difference of the greatest kind. I have heard many non-believers make the statement that Christians are no different from them. I pray that no one can ever say that about my life, not because I'm perfect, but because the light and love Christ resides within me.

2 Timothy 1:9
Who has saved us, and called us with a holy calling, not according to our works, but according to His own purpose and grace which was granted us in Christ Jesus from all eternity. – NASB

If we who have accepted salvation, are no different that those who have not. How mute is our testimony? Instead of showing the world the light of heaven, we have just tossed another match upon the lake of fire. We must seek God's wisdom daily, so we will not bring shame to His name.

Colossians 3:9-11
**Do not lie to one another, since you laid aside the old self with
its evil practices, and have put on the new self who is being
renewed to a true knowledge according to the image of the One
who created him. A renewal in which there is no distinction
between Greek and Jew, circumcised and uncircumcised,
barbarian, Scythian, slave and freeman, <u>but Christ is all, and
in all</u>. –NASB**

Christ's salvation that we accepted freely from God our
Heavenly Father has transformed us into a new creation. Because
Christ lives in us, we must love righteousness and hate sin. Anger
of the flesh is a sin that not only harms us physically, it also
crushes our spirit and can hurt those around us. If therefore, we
are children of God, then we should despise sin. Christ came into
the world so that we **<u>ALL</u>** might have life. If we profess to be one
with him, then we too must bring forth life. That life does not
come from our flesh, but from our spirits. The instrument of life
and death is our tongue. The next time you face these situations,
make a forced effort like an army taking ground in a battle to
respond with life instead of death. Be mindful of all your ways for
God is watching, and it is the believer who will have to give an
account for his or her actions.

Philippians 2:14-16
**Do all things without grumbling or disputing; that you may
prove yourselves to be blameless and innocent, children of God
above reproach in the midst of a crooked and perverse
generation, among whom you appear as lights in the world,
holding fast the word of life, so that in the day of Christ I may**

Glenda C. Finkelstein

have cause to glory because I did not run in vain nor toil in vain. – NASB

<u>Chapter Three</u>

The good, the rude, and the indifferent...

You have safely arrived at work or school on this beautiful, fantastic Monday morning! Yes, Monday morning the beginning of the week, but you cringe at the thought of Monday. After all, that means five long days of dealing with that irritating boss. Not to mention that lazy thing your boss calls your co-worker, whose only interest is seeing how much work they don't have to do than getting the job done. Let's not forget that overbearing throwback of a teacher that loathes the day you were born. The menageries of personalities that you must work with, learn from, or just flat be exposed to can be overwhelming.

I don't believe that every person we come into contact with is a terrible person. I know that all of us can think of at least one person that makes it difficult for us to maintain our Christianity. In fact, there are people out there that can make us get into the flesh so fast that all we have to do is think of them. These are the people you have a hard enough time just being in the same room with, but your Christian walk demands that you love these people as yourself. How can you love someone you don't even like? How can you love someone who hates you? Difficult questions, but just like our other mountains this too will move only by prayer and reading the word.

Christ commanded that we pray for our enemies. This was not a suggestion, or a simple please keep me from my enemy kind of prayer. Christ came for the lost, the perishing, and the outcast. If He were to come to your place of employment, who do you think He would take to lunch? You, or your enemy? My vote is for the one who needs Him. You already know Him, but there is much to gain for the kingdom of God to bring a lost sheep back into the fold. We can't be selective Christians doing only those things that make us feel comfortable. We must transform our minds to think the way Christ thinks.

Luke 6:27-36
But I say to you who hear: Love your enemies, do good to those who hate you, bless those who curse you, and pray for those who spitefully use you. To him who strikes you on one cheek, offer the other also. And from him who takes away your cloak, do not withhold your tunic either. Give to everyone who asks of you. And from him who takes away your goods do not ask them back. And just as you want men to do to you, you also do to them likewise. But if you love those who love you, what credit is that to you? For even sinners love those who love them. And if you do good to those who do good to you. What credit is that to you? For even sinners do the same. And if you lend to those from whom you hope to receive back, what credit

is that to you? For even sinners lend to sinners to receive as much back.

But love your enemies, do good, and lend, hoping for nothing in return; and your reward will be great, and you will be the son of the Most High. For He is kind to the unthankful and evil. Therefore be merciful, just as your Father also is merciful. – NKJV

As a Christian this is probably one of the most difficult things to do. For a long time, I thought that we were to become victims, but that is so far from the truth. First of all, He didn't call us to make bad choices in the people we choose as friends. He is referring to those that we didn't choose to interact with like in the office, the classroom, or the grocery store. There is nothing that a thief can take from you that God can't replace or restore. It's not worth losing your life for a purse, a garment, or a piece of jewelry. All of these things you can replace. Dealing with thieves is becoming more commonplace as technology evolves. Regardless, we tend to deal with the large traumatic experiences better than we do an everyday, irritating, ordinary one.

A thief is only one kind of enemy, whose biggest casualty is a violation of trust and security. There are others in our lives that you might not think of as an enemy, but then again anyone you don't like is an enemy. I realize that enemy is a strong word with visions of armies in battle, but if they are not your friend or acquaintance and you know them, then by default they must be an enemy. These could be people that just rub you the wrong way.

31

Glenda C. Finkelstein

They could be cheaters, selfish individuals, religious hypocrites, or just plain rude, crude, and unacceptable. I could go on, but I think you get the idea. These are the very ones that you need to witness to, but haven't been able to because you just don't want to deal with them. Perhaps you have tried, but to no avail and the best you have come to expect is to avoid arguing with them. Take heart and be of good cheer because you are about to enter into a golden nugget of God's truth. You are not alone.

2 Corinthians 4:7-9
But we have this treasure in earthen vessels, <u>that the surpassing greatness of the</u> power may be of God and not from ourselves; we are afflicted in every way, but not crushed; perplexed, but not despairing; persecuted, but not forsaken, struck down, but not destroyed. –NASB

We will face enemies, hardships, and just plain difficulties, but God is always with us. When you pray for your enemies, you need to separate them from their sin. See them as God sees them. Look at the sinner, not the sin. Pray for them with all your heart that God will move on their behalf to remove the painful hidden scars that have made them that way. If they are unkind to you, respond with kindness no matter how much it hurts. This is something that you must do consistently regardless if you see any change. Otherwise, they will think your kind response was because you were on drugs or something. They <u>need</u> to see Christ in you.

32

Don't just pray for them, pray for yourself that God will allow you to see them through His eyes.

Romans 12:20-21
Therefore "If your enemy hungers, feed him; If he thirsts, give him a drink; For in so doing you will heap coals of fire on his head." Do not be overcome by evil, but overcome evil with good. – NKJV

You might this scripture is contradictory when it speaks of heaping burning coals on someone's head. Quite the contrary this was actually an act of hospitality so that when a person returned to their home at night they would have hot coals to start their fire, but not everyone chooses to follow God or do the right thing. Regardless, you must show kindness to your enemies. For some, these actions will bring them into repentance, for others that reject your efforts' justice will not go unserved. Your reward is from God, not from men. Keep in mind that this is not your struggle or even your decision as to whether mercy or justice is the proper reward. This has nothing to do with you and everything to do with the power of the Holy Spirit. It is not our calling to judge them. Our call is to love them with a love that does not come from ourselves, but from Christ.

Proverbs 25:21-22
If your enemy is hungry, give him bread to eat; And if he is thirsty, give him water to drink; For so you will heap coals of fire on his head, and the Lord will reward you. – NKJV

Yes, I am harping on this point. We, as children of God, must be different and show our Father's love regardless of the circumstances. Again, if our enemies respond to that love, God will use us to draw them unto Him. If they resist that love and continue in their ways, then we will receive our reward and be protected from them. Don't be kind to your enemies expecting something kind in return from them. Remember your reward is from God, not from men. This is not something, however, that we can do in our own strength. The moment you take one step on your own, you will fall. Pray for the Lord's strength and guidance for He will not let us stand alone.

Malachi 3:6
For I am the Lord, I do not change; Therefore, you are not consumed, O sons of Jacob. – NKJV

A few years ago, I had a real situation with a fellow employee of a past employer who made me feel very uncomfortable by action and word. This person's actions would count as those of an enemy bringing harm upon me rather than good. I went through all the human processes of filing reports to my managers, etc. The human procedures did not work. It wasn't until I started praying for that person every day for God to move in

34

this person's life, that I began to see some change. This change, however, did not happen immediately.

I prayed for this person every day for a couple of months. I wasn't sure what this would do exactly except for the fact that God commanded that we do this, but as the days went on things got better. Later, I found out this person would be taking a position of authority over me, and I became worried. Even though I knew God was there, I felt very strongly that He did not want me to stay there. This situation was very stressful on me personally, and I needed to feel at peace with my job, so I posted out for another position. In the meantime, he was my authority. During this time, I made every effort to conduct myself with respect to his position avoiding any one on one situations. He was not unaware of the displeasure I had for his actions towards me, and seemed to respect my actions of professionalism. Before leaving, however, this individual became a supporter of my professional attitudes and was even willing to provide a glowing letter of recommendation for my next boss.

Things like this don't just happen without God. To take a person who was intent on doing me harm, and turn them completely around to supporting me was nothing less than a miracle. It was not easy for me to pray for this person because they had hurt me, but I had a commandment from God to love this person. For me, obedience was the only way to go. Through these prayers, I began to see this person as they really were, an

Glenda C. Finkelstein

individual which Christ gave His life to save. When I told my best
friend about these events, she quoted the following scripture to me.

Proverbs 16:7
**When a man's ways please the Lord, He makes even his
enemies to be at peace with him. – NKJV**

There was a time that we were an enemy of God, and yet
He still sent his Son to die for our sins. For those of us who know
Him, can we truly withhold God's love and kindness from the very
ones He came to save? His will is that none should perish. It is
very easy to sing a song in church about reaching the lost, and
quite another to extend a hand of generosity to those who irritate or
despise you. To get to the very heart of the matter, it isn't about us
it's about Jesus Christ, the one who can make a way where there
was no way. There are so many ways we can show the love of
God to others. We don't need to stand on top of our desks yelling
"Repent for the kingdom of God is at hand!" We just need to walk
the talk and humble ourselves in prayer seeking His wisdom.
Open your heart to the burden of the Lord for the lost. See them
through Spirit eyes and reach out with random acts of kindness
done in sincere love.

Joel 2:12-13
**"Yet even now," declares the Lord, "Return to Me with all
your heart, and with fasting, weeping and mourning; And rend
your heart and not your garments." Now return to the Lord**

your God, for He is gracious and compassionate, slow to anger, abounding in loving kindness, and relenting of evil. –NASB

I would like for you to take just a moment and think of someone who causes you great irritation. Get their face firmly planted in your mind's eye. Now step back and see your Lord and Savior looking down from Calvary with blood and tears flowing from His brow. Look into His face now swollen and bruised. Hear Him speak those awesome words of forgiveness in the darkest hour eternity has ever known.

Luke 23:34
But Jesus was saying, "Father, forgive them; for they do not know what they are doing." And they cast lots, dividing up His garments among themselves. –NASB

Return now to the person in your mind's eye and see them in the shadow of the cross. You and I are no different from them. For all of humanity stood at the foot of the cross that day stained with the guilt of sin. The sins we committed which pierced our Lord on Calvary are no less vile than the sinner you see in your mind's eye now. You, however, have experienced salvation and are not the person you once were. If God showed us forgiveness, how can we not forgive and love with the same mercy?

Romans 5:8-10
But God demonstrates His own love toward us, in that while we were yet sinners, Christ died for us. Much more then,

having now been justified by His blood we shall be saved from the wrath of God through Him. For if while we were enemies, we were reconciled to God through the death of His Son, much more, having been reconciled, we shall be saved by His life. – NASB

Since we are children of God, His Spirit dwells in each one of us His church. Not a day should go by that we do not put on the full armor of God so that we will stand firm in the face of adversity. Our God that is in us will not leave us nor forsake us ever. His is the strength to love, His is the mercy of forgiveness, and we are His bearers of the light of His glory and grace.

Romans 8:35-39
Who shall separate us from the love of Christ? Shall tribulation, or distress, or persecution, or famine, or nakedness, or peril, or sword? As it is written: "For Your sake we are killed all day long. We are accounted as sheep for the slaughter." Yet in all these things we are more than conquerors through Him who loved us. For I am persuaded that neither death nor life, nor angels nor principalities nor powers, nor things present nor things to come, nor height nor depth, nor any other created thing, shall be able to separate us from the love of God which is in Christ Jesus our Lord. – NKJV

Know then that the Lord our God is faithful, and if we will just be obedient to His commandments we will overcome our own flesh. Will we have to change? Yes. Will we have to die to self? Yes. Do we have to show love to the loveless? Yes. Do we have to forgive those who harm us? Yes. Do we have to give to anyone who asks? Yes. None of these things we can or shall do out of our own strength, but through our Savior, Jesus Christ.

Philippians 4:13
I can do all things through Christ who strengthens me. –
NKJV

Glenda C. Finkelstein

Chapter Four

Fat Phantom vs. Heavenly Manna

All of the day's routines can make one very hungry. What shall we eat, is a question that plagues every American? There are diets for calorie counters, fat grams, carbohydrates, heart smart, bone smart, cancer smart, regularity smart, and any other thing you can imagine. My goodness, there seems to be no end. So what should a person eat?

I grew up in the South where people could cook, and cook well. I have memories of family reunions where we would feast on spareribs, wonderful salads, vegetables, breads, and the decadent desserts that would always follow them. Sunday dinners of chicken and dumplings, roast beef and gravy, and homemade biscuits make my mouth water just thinking about them. I could go on, but these days it's almost a sin to eat something that isn't completely fat free, calorie free, sodium free, and flavor free. I don't recall God saying I have made air for you to eat.

Glenda C. Finkelstein

The best piece of advice I can give for food intake for our physical bodies is what my mother ingrained into my being all of my life. Eat a balanced meal. Don't over indulge in any one type of food. Eat a variety of fruits, vegetables, meats, breads, and yes you can have a dessert just don't go overboard.

Our spirit requires nourishment just like our physical man, and just like our physical man too much or not enough of the right things can be detrimental. Our spirit receives a daily bombardment of the world from television, magazines, newspapers, and the news (which I affectionately call the daily morgue report). What our spirit needs is a daily meal of the living word of God. Not many of us would purposely deprive our physical man of the nutrients it needs, so why do we so willingly deprive our spirit man of the Bible.

Matthew 4:4
But He answered and said, "It is written, Man shall not live on bread alone, but on every word that proceeds out of the mouth of God." – NASB

During a time of testing, Christ quotes the living word of God to Satan. Christ had fasted for forty days and nights, and did not succumb to His flesh. Even though His body hungered, His spirit knew that God's word not only brings life, but is life.

Deuteronomy 8:3
And He humbled you and let you be hungry, and fed you with
manna which you did not know, nor did your fathers know,
that He might make you understand that man does not live by
bread alone, but man lives by everything that proceeds out of
the mouth of the Lord. –NASB

Here God is reminding His people of the provision which
He provided in the wilderness after He had delivered them from
Egypt. They had to learn that by the Word of His promises He
would keep them, and by their obedience to His word they would
prosper. Our history is full of examples where man has lived and
died over words. How many martyrs have died whose only
comfort was His word? What risks do some even today take just
to hear the good news of the gospel? Yet, we who have God's
word at our fingertips seldom open it.

It's no wonder that we feel defeated, drained, and unhappy.
Our spirit man is starving to death. When are the children of God
going to realize that it is our obedience to the word of God that
builds faith? Obedience to prayer that increases endurance, and
obedience to praise that will bring forth joy. God's word is perfect
for yesterday, today, and tomorrow. It is not just a collection of
stories. The Bible is full of many treasures such as
encouragement, provision, hope, salvation, protection, and truth.
The power of God is in His word.

Glenda C. Finkelstein

John 1:1-5
**In the beginning was the Word, and the Word was with God,
and the Word was God. He was in the beginning with God.
All things came into being by Him, and apart from Him
nothing came into being that has come into being. In Him was
life and the life was the light of men. And the light shines in
the darkness, and the darkness did not comprehend it. – NASB**

These words are a testimony to the great I AM of the

Trinity. He is everything. Apart from Him even we are nothing

but an empty void. Our survival depends upon Him. You might

say that this is all very nice, but the world seems to be doing just

fine outside of God's grace. There are people living around you

every day that don't seem to need God's word and many of them

are successful people with nice homes, cars, etc.. I would have to

agree that there are many people who are like that, but what they

have is temporary. A thief can break into your house and steel. A

storm can destroy it in seconds. Cars can meet the same fates.

Take away their possessions and what do you have? You have

nothing but chaff being blown away by the wind.

Luke 6:24
**But woe to you who are rich, for you are receiving your
comfort in full. – NASB**

Do you know what the difference is between a successful

person and a blessed person? The successful person can precisely

dictate how they achieved every dollar they have accumulated.

They also tend to complain about the weight of its management. A
44

blessed person knows that what they have is a gift from God's throne, and if it disappeared tomorrow they still have their blessing because God is with them. They are also more than willing to give to anyone else who has need.

Isaiah 55:2-3
Why do you spend money for what is not bread, and your wages for what does not satisfy? Listen carefully to Me, and eat what is good, and delight yourself in abundance. <u>Incline your ear and come to Me. Listen, that you may live</u>; and I will make an everlasting covenant with you, according to the faithful mercies shown to David. – NASB

The world desperately searches for things that will satisfy their needs, and are still empty. Drugs, money, vacations, careers, hobbies, sports, relationships, cars, and food are only a few of the things the world seeks. The list is endless of what the world offers to those who are seeking fulfillment and a meaning for their lives. All of these things promise so much and deliver so little. Even Christians lose their way and seek after these vain things. Anything that becomes more important to you than your relationship with God is an idol. God will bring it down with or without your repentance. Fortunately, a true child of God who acquires understanding does not need to chase after such things.

Glenda C. Finkelstein

Matthew 6:25
For this reason I say to you, do not be anxious for your life, as to what you shall eat, or what you shall drink; nor for your body, as to what you shall put on. Is not life more than food, and the body than clothing? – NASB

We spend a lot of our time wondering what we are going to eat, and what we are going to wear. Instead we should be thanking God for His provision, and show that thankfulness by sharing what we have with others. That's right, be thankful for what you have, and give accordingly knowing that the true owner of all that we have is our Heavenly Father. There are times I have fallen into the trap that if we just get to this level of financial status we can do this for God.

Allow me to let you in on a little secret. God has enabled you to give something be it money, food, clothing, service, prayer, or time. Each of us can do for God right where we are in God.

Mark 12:41-44
And He sat down opposite the treasury, and began observing how the multitude were putting money into the treasury; and many rich people were putting in large sums. And a poor widow came and put in two small copper coins, which amount to a cent. And calling His disciples to Him, He said to them, "Truly I say to you, this poor widow put in more than all the contributors to the treasury; for they all put in out of their surplus, but she, out of her poverty, put in all she owned, all she had to live on." – NASB

The Bible doesn't elaborate on the widow who gave out of faith where she was and all she had, but the eyes of heaven were upon her that day. I have no doubt that she received a very rich reward and that she did not know want. How many times did Christ say that your faith has made you whole when he touched the sick to heal them? Faith doesn't stop with just one need or circumstance.

Luke 6:38
Give, and it will be given to you; good measure, pressed down, shaken together, running over, they will pour into your lap. <u>For by your standard of measure</u> it will be measured to you in return. – NASB

Please note that it says by our measure it will return. That widow gave all. I'll let you do the math. Sometimes it frustrates me living here in America. Instead of being grateful and sharing from our abundance, we become brats who are selfish and complain about things that mean nothing. There are countless millions of people who must steal or kill simply for the crust of bread that you tossed into the garbage because you were too full to eat another bite.

Don't misunderstand me I'm not asking you to feel guilty for eating your meal, but I am asking that you appreciate every single bite that goes into your mouth. I am asking that the next time someone asks you to give to anyone that has a greater need than yourself that you will give generously. Even if it means not

47

buying that extra pair of shoes that is perfect for your new dress, or maybe it's that computer software that you just have to have. It can wait one more payday. There is a need in God's kingdom that we must meet today. Christ came to feed the hungry in body and spirit. Can we afford to do any less? Perhaps God's word can explain it far better than I.

1 Thessalonians 1:2-6
We give thanks to God always for all of you, making mention of you in our prayers; constantly bearing in mind your work of faith and labor of love and steadfastness of hope in our Lord Jesus Christ in the presence of our God and Father, knowing, brethren beloved by God, His choice of you; for our gospel did not come to you in word only, but also in power and in the Holy Spirit and with full conviction; just as you know what kind of men we proved to be among you for your sake. You also became imitators of us and of the Lord, having received the word in much tribulation with the joy of the Holy Spirit. – NASB

God's word is so much more than just a word whether spoken or written. God's spoken word carries with it the power of creation. The power to speak into existence life and light belongs to God alone.

Genesis 1:3
Then God said, "Let there be light" ; and there was light. – NKJV

By His word He grants forgiveness through the word, that was Christ, who died for our sins. Where we broke the covenant with God, He restored it by His Promise.

Hebrews 10:15-18
And the Holy Spirit also bears witness to us; for after saying, "This is the covenant that I will make with them after those days, says the Lord; I will put my laws upon their heart, and upon their mind I will write them," He then says, "And their sins and their lawless deeds I will remember no more." Now where there is forgiveness of these things, there is no longer any offering for sin. – NASB

Through God's word, He gives us other promises of protection, provision, healing, and many, many more. No matter what your circumstances, God has a promise to deliver you. You will never know what they are unless you read the word. It is difficult to claim something that you don't even know exists.

2 Peter 1:4
For by these He has granted to us His precious and magnificent promises, in order that by them you might become partakers of the divine nature, having escaped the corruption that is in the world by lust. – NASB

God's word carries the benefit of eternal life. It is our pardon from judgment. Our corruption covered by the perfect and final sacrifice for Sin, given by the Lamb. The eternal word of Love that is perfect in our Heavenly Father.

John 5:24

Truly, truly I say to you, he who hears My word, and believes Him who sent Me has eternal life, and does not come into judgment, but has passed out of death into life. – NASB

The next time you grab a bag of chips to munch on consider picking up the Bible and feasting upon the words of God. Just as you would share your snack with a friend, share what God imparts to a friend as well. His word is food for the hungry, drink for the thirsty, and life for the perishing.

Matthew 5:14-16
You are the light of the world. A city set on a hill cannot be hidden. Nor do men light a lamp and put it under a basket, but on a lamp stand; and it gives light to all who are in the house. Let your light shine before men in such a way that they may see your good works, and glorify your Father who is in heaven. – NASB

<u>Chapter Five</u>

Mistakes, Errors, and Oops. Oh my!

We are humans and as humans we are born in sin. Even those of us that have experienced the saving Grace of God are not perfect. We will make mistakes. It is not surprising to know that some days are better than others, and by our own admission should have stayed in bed. We still venture forth bravely, foolishly, and unwisely approaching our days using only our own strength. These are the days that are prime targets for making huge and grandiose mistakes. Words spoken out of anger, actions not thought through, and pride humbled to the level of embarrassment. We were doing so well, too. How could we have allowed ourselves to mess up so badly?

How can we profess to be a follower of Christ when our example is plunging into the depths of the mud? Why is it that when we, Christians, make a mistake or fall into temptation that it is so much worse than those that are not? Perhaps, it is because we know better and hopefully in most cases have done better. Humble

Glenda C. Finkelstein

pie is very bitter, but it also removes any scales of personal grandeur from our eyes. It is at these times that we see the clearest just how much we need our Savior.

How then do we recover from such a time? We must be cautious when recovering from a mistake. The enemy can use these experiences to keep us down or discredit our witness to others. Our failure can become the basket that covers our light, but it doesn't have to stay there. The first thing we must do is ask for forgiveness, and realize that we are not the only ones who have ever made a mistake.

Romans 3:23
For <u>all</u> have sinned and fall short of the glory of God. – NKJV

Please note that the word "all" means everybody, but just because we are in a large group of people does not mean that we shouldn't strive to do better. We should not use it as an excuse to continue in a sin that the Holy Spirit has already convicted you. Understand that convicted and condemned are two very different things. Conviction simply means that you have sinned; you are aware that it is a sin, and you are being called to forsake it for holiness.

I John 2:1-2
My little children, I am writing these things to you that you may not sin. And if anyone sins, we have an Advocate with the Father, Jesus Christ the righteous; and He Himself is the

propitiation for our sins' and not for ours only, but also for those of the whole world. – NASB

One thing that I have noticed in the Bible is that, even though, the humans in it are not perfect, God still maintained His plan. The people whom He chose to use in those plans may have gotten off the beaten path from time to time, but God's plan didn't. Samson is one such individual that comes to mind. He at times became so prideful and lustful it is difficult to see how he could do anything for God. God chose him from conception to deliver the people of Israel from the Philistines. Despite Samson's weakness, God's plan still came to fruition. If Samson had been more obedient, he probably would have had greater blessings and a longer life.

Another example is the promise that David's line would produce the Messiah. The kings that followed David came dangerously close to destroying that plan, but in spite of them all God fulfilled His plan and His promise.

I am not saying that we shouldn't strive to better ourselves or correct our errors because God will always accomplish His plan. God abhors sin, and we His children should also. All I am saying is that when we make a mistake, we cause damage, but it is not irreparable. We can recover, but we have to get back up on our feet and knock the dust off our pants. We have to give over to God what we cannot do alone, and we have to take responsibility for making it good by confessing and reconciling. Don't let the

Glenda C. Finkelstein

enemy trick you into thinking that you can make a mistake and run away from it, or that God will hold it against you for the rest of your life. If you come before God with a true, repentant heart, He will not only forgive, but forget.

Jeremiah 31:34
"And they shall not teach again, each man his neighbor and each man his brother, saying, 'Know the Lord,' for they shall all know Me, from the least of them to the greatest of them," declares the Lord, "for I will forgive their iniquity, and their sin I will remember no more." – NASB

The Lord is ready to forgive, but you must come to Him with a repentant heart. It is not enough to ease your guilty conscience by saying you're sorry. You must be willing to <u>do</u> what is necessary to make restitution for the wrong you have done. In other words, you must be ready to make a change. For some this may mean forsaking a temptation, for others this may mean reconciling themselves to a brother where words have placed a wall of separation. Whatever our mistakes might be, we must be willing to change our lives so restoration can take place. We have made many mistakes, but through all of them God's love did not change.

Psalm 86:1-5
Incline Thine ear, O Lord, and answer me; For I am afflicted and needy. Do preserve my soul, for I am a godly man; O Thou my God, save Thy servant who trusts in Thee. Be gracious to me, O Lord, For to Thee I cry all day long. Make glad the soul of Thy servant, For to Thee, O Lord, I lift up my
54

soul. <u>**For Thou, Lord, art good, and ready to forgive, And abundant in loving kindness to all who call upon Thee.**</u> **– NASB**

When it comes to making mistakes or bad decisions there are many things that come into play. Reaping and sowing for instance is a natural law. You will reap the results of the sin that you have sown. Many times it is the reaping process that causes us to repent. Yet, if we are truly repentant God will grant mercy and grace to ease the consequences of our actions leaving enough to teach us discipline, or leave a bad enough taste in our mouths so we'll have no desire to repeat the experience.

Galatians 6: 7-8
Do not be deceived, God is not mocked; for whatever a man sows, this he will also reap. For the one who sows to his own flesh shall from the flesh reap corruption, but the one who sows to the Spirit shall from the Spirit reap eternal life. – NASB

God is a God of justice. We must learn the true wages of our actions. Some of these lessons come with a higher cost than we realized when we committed our wrong. Yet even in the midst of this process God is willing and able to forgive. Draw nearer to God. Don't allow your mistake to turn you away from God. Instead turn to Him and humble yourself. He is merciful. Take that mercy and reconcile to the one you have wronged.

Romans 4: 7-8

Glenda C. Finkelstein

Blessed are those whose lawless deeds have been forgiven, and whose sins have been covered. Blessed is the man whose sin the Lord will not take into account. – NASB

What is that you say? You are the victim. Then you are the one who must forgive. I know that you think that is it easy for me to tell you this, because I do not know your pain. I have never suffered loss as you have suffered loss, but neither to you know my suffering. I, being human, am not naturally willing to forgive those who have hurt me either. Yet, I must forgive because God demands it from His children.

Matthew 6:14-15
For if you forgive men for their transgressions, your heavenly Father will also forgive you. But if you do not forgive men, then your Father will not forgive your transgressions. – NASB

That is a bitter pill to swallow. How can you forgive someone who has caused you pain? It's easier to forgive a small thing, but what about the drunk driver who took your child's life? The man who defiled you? The man or woman who betrayed you? How do you forgive the person that abused your child? How can God forgive us for doing the same thing to His Son? I'm sure you think I just jumped off into the deep end of the pool. We never did anything to Christ! If you have committed any sin, you have done it to the Lord. In spite of that, he still loves us because His is a perfect love. When we accept the sacrifice of His Son, we will also perfect our love for ourselves and others.

56

Isaiah 40:27-31
**Why do you say, O Jacob, and assert, O Israel, "My way is
hidden from the Lord, And the justice due me escapes the
notice of my God?" Do you not know? Have you not heard?
The everlasting God, the Lord, the Creator of the ends of the
earth does not become weary or tired. His understanding is
inscrutable. He gives strength to the weary, and to him who
lacks might He increases power. Though youths grow weary
and tired, and vigorous young men stumble badly, Yet those
who wait for the Lord will gain new strength; They will mount
up with wings like eagles, They will run and not get tired, They
will walk and not become weary. – NASB**

God loves the sinner and hates the sin. When you forgive
you are granting a pardon for the sinner and in so doing a pardon
for yourself. As much as we hate to accept or admit it, we are
corruptible seed. It is Christ in us that can transform that
corruption into incorruptible seed pleasing to God. Without
Christ, we cannot come before God and please Him in any way.

Forgiveness is a blessing and is the beginning of healing
and deliverance, but only love can forgive. Hate does not, envy
does not, hurt does not, and selfishness does not. Non-forgiveness
hardens the heart and keeps it in bondage and apart from God.
Some may say that only God can forgive some people because
their sin was so bad. I would have to say that on our own strength
we cannot, but with God's help we can. If Christ could forgive us,
the ones who brought him to Calvary, we must forgive others. Are
we so holy that we can't remember our own darkness? Were we

worthy of Salvation as the sinner we were before Christ? Are we so arrogant to think that our hands are innocent because we were not there that day?

Love is what allowed Himself to hang on the cross for our sins. Love is what overcame hell and the grave. The perfect love of God is what came to us because we could not go to Him. He gave us all. He removed Himself from Glory to become a man that we could see, touch, and hear on the hope that we would come home. He made the sacrifice that we were unable to make so that we could come back into fellowship with Him. It was not man's authority that made the sacrifice, but God's authority.

Matthew 26:51-56
And behold, one of those who were with Jesus reached and drew out his sword, and struck the slave of the high priest and cut off his ear. Then Jesus said to him, "Put your sword back into its place; for all those who take up the sword shall perish by the sword. Or do you think that I cannot appeal to My Father, and He will at once put at My disposal more than twelve legions of angels? How then will the Scriptures be fulfilled, which say that it must happen this way?" At that time Jesus said to the multitudes, "Have you come out with swords and clubs to arrest Me as against a robber? Every day I used to sit in the temple teaching and you did not seize Me. But all this has taken place that the scriptures of the prophets may be fulfilled." Then all the disciples left Him and fled. – NASB

Christ was far from helpless and chose to do His Father's will to fulfill the scriptures. To this end, he made one perfect and complete sacrifice for the forgiveness of sins, washing them away

as if they never were so that we could come home. Accepting
Jesus Christ has brought us into a love that the world does not
know or understand. Following God's will instead of your own is
not easy. It was not easy for Christ. In Gethsemane before the
men came to arrest him, He was in such earnest prayer that
droplets of blood fell from his forehead.

Luke 22:41-44
**And He withdrew from them about a stone's throw, and He
knelt down and began to pray saying, "Father, if Thou art
willing, remove this cup from Me; yet not My will, but Thine
be done." Now an angel from heaven appeared to Him
strengthening Him. And being in agony He was praying very
fervently; and His sweat became like drops of blood, falling
down upon the ground. – NASB**

Everything we do must be in the Father's will. It is at
times very difficult because we can't see past the night or the
circumstances that surround us, but Christ was not to remain dead
or defeated. In the midst of this seemingly hopeless circumstance,
God made the impossible possible.

Matthew 28:1-7
**Now after the Sabbath, as it began to dawn toward the first
day of the week, Mary Magdalene and the other Mary came to
look at the grave. And behold, a severe earthquake had
occurred for an angel of the Lord descended from heaven and
came and rolled away the stone and sat upon it. And his
appearance was like lightning and his garment as white as
snow; and the guards shook for fear of him, and became like
dead men. And the angel answered and said to the women,
"Do not be afraid; for I know that you are looking for Jesus**

who has been crucified. He is not here, for He has risen, just as He said. Come, see the place where He was lying. And go quickly and tell His disciples that He has risen from the dead, and behold is going on before you into Galilee, there you will see Him; behold I have told you." – NASB

In the same way that Christ's resurrection raised Him from the dead. Forgiveness resurrects those things that were dead in your spirit. It brings new life, and reconciliation between you and God. It is the ultimate expression of love because you have to sacrifice a piece of yourself. It is time to crush the pity party of woe is me I am hurting, or I have made a mistake. Christ didn't die and overcome hell and the grave for you to wallow in self-pity. He did these things so that we could overcome our own humanity and love one another as He loves us.

2 Corinthians 5:17-21
Therefore if any man is in Christ, he is a new creature; the old things passed away; behold, new things have come. Now all these things are from God, who reconciled us to Himself through Christ, and gave us the ministry of reconciliation, namely, that God was in Christ reconciling the world to Himself, <u>not counting their trespasses against them</u>, and He has committed to us the word of reconciliation. Therefore, we are ambassadors for Christ, as though God were entreating through us; we beg you on behalf of Christ, be reconciled to God. He made Him who knew no sin to be sin on our behalf that we might become the righteousness of God in Him. – NASB

Remember that God's love is there even when we make a mistake. He knows your heart. Let Him be your Heavenly Father. His hands and arms are open and ready to pick you up and set you on a new path. He has made plans for your life, plans that will prosper you and bring glory to His kingdom. Return to your prayer closet. Return to reading the word of God daily. Return to praising His name for the little things in your life regardless if the day is sunny or stormy. You may only see up to the horizon, but God sees eternity.

Psalm 37:23-24
The steps of a good man are ordered by the Lord, and He delights in his way. Though he fall, he shall not be utterly cast down; for the Lord upholds him with His hand. – NKJV

Glenda C. Finkelstein

Chapter Six

Traffic Jams

It is rush hour, and you are on your way home. You have survived the day, but it's not over until you have arrived safely at home. You get into your car and drive full speed ahead into the nightly traffic jam. The lane beside you is moving, but you are standing still. You finally make it into the moving lane just in time to stop and watch the one you just left start to move. Suddenly you get a great idea! You will take the side street over on the left. Surely no one knows that street will go through to the one you need. You take the chance and at first things are moving right along. Then you find yourself fast approaching the brake lights of another car. You hit the brakes and find yourself stuck again. Even the snail on the side of the road seems to be passing you.

It's so frustrating when you become trapped by those traffic jams, and people are honking their horns like that is actually going to make this move any faster, while everyone sits in their car going at the breakneck speed of ZERO MPH! Out of frustration, you

Glenda C. Finkelstein

honk your horn which gives a brief moment of satisfaction, but ultimately ends up adding to the already noisy throng of stressed out drivers.

Many times our lives resemble a traffic jam more than anything else. It seems as if everyone else is getting and doing while we are just waiting for something to happen in our own lives as if watching the parade passing us by. We wait for the house to be paid off, wait for the kids to grow up, or just feel stuck in a job you can't stand. You go to the store and wait in the checkout line. Everywhere you turn you seem to be waiting for something. It can be a very frustrating and empty time, but many times God has instructed us to wait on Him. What's that you say? You mean I have to wait on God too! Yes, but don't lose you're cool it's a good thing, really.

Psalm 27:14
Wait for the Lord; be strong, and let your heart take courage; Yes, wait for the Lord. – NASB

There is a powerful strength found in the patience of waiting. It allows us to thoroughly understand the cost of what we are trying to attain. It allows us time to plan and make decisions without the hindrance of erratic emotions. Waiting gives us the clarity of thought to separate our purpose from our whims. It's also a time for counting the blessings that we have been given and appreciate them.

Psalm 37:34
Wait for the Lord, and keep His way, and He will exalt you to inherit the land; When the wicked are cut off, you will see it. – NASB

There are blessings in waiting on God, but why does He instruct us to wait? I believe the answer to this is much simpler than one might imagine. Let's take children as an example. Whether you have one of your own or not, we have all been a child and can relate to this scenario. A child wants everything now! As a parent, this has been my most frustrating lesson to teach my child. You can't always have everything right now. Even good things have a proper time and place. A child may want a cookie now, but they need to eat their meal first. Otherwise, the treat may take away their hunger for nourishment. The treat is not bad, but at the wrong time can become bad.

God many times will withhold blessings, our cookies because He knows that we must have the nourishment of reading the word, praying, fasting, and increasing our faith. If these things do not come first, we will lose our appetite for the things of God, and we would squander His blessings. God wants only the best for his children.

Now that you have an example of waiting, I am sure you can think of many more. Our life is full of waiting. There are several statistics out about the amount of time we spend waiting in lines. It's quite disturbing to think about how much time we spend waiting, but how we wait is far more important than what we're waiting to receive? The word "wait" is a verb. A verb denotes action. Waiting is not simply passing the time until we get what we want. In the above example with the cookie, the child was not simply waiting because there was no reason beyond aggravation. The child was waiting because there is an order that promotes the best results for his or her physical health.

Luke 12:36-37
And be like men who are waiting for their master when he returns from the wedding feast, so that they may immediately open the door to him when he comes and knocks. Blessed are those slaves whom the master shall find on the alert when he comes; truly I say to you that he will gird himself to serve and have them recline at the table, and will come up and wait on them. – NASB

The word "wait" also denotes a state of readiness. Waiting should be a time of preparation. We should be in a state of readiness so when the call to action sounds we can meet the challenge before us. In the example of the child with the cookie, if he didn't wait for the cookie eating it first, he would have lost his appetite. His energy level would not sustain him for very long becoming too tired to enjoy the experiences offered that day. By eating the cookie after his meal, it served as a reward allowing him to meet all of the day's challenges.

We Christians get so excited when we receive a revelation from God or feel a calling upon our lives that we sometimes try to grab the cookie before the meal. Yet we cannot let ourselves be swept up in the emotion of the moment that we venture forth without waiting and exercising that time of preparation. God is patient and waits on us to learn, grow, and mature. There are many saints that have gone on before us, and we should learn to trust God's perfect timing.

Isaiah 30:18
Therefore the Lord longs to be gracious to you, and therefore He waits on high to have compassion on you. For the Lord is a God of justice; How blessed are all those who long for Him. – NASB

God has set aside a time of waiting to prepare you for the task He has chosen for you. Do not let your time of waiting be filled with grumbling and coveting the lives of those who are in a different place in their walk. Sometimes we must walk together, and sometimes we must take different roads. If it is your time of waiting, do so with joy, praise, thankfulness, and seeking God's face.

Proverbs 8:17-21
"I love those who love Me, and those who diligently seek Me will find Me. Riches and honor are with Me. Enduring wealth and righteousness. My fruit is better than gold, even pure gold, and My yield than choicest silver. I walk in the way of righteousness, In the midst of the paths of justice, to endow those who love Me with wealth, that I may fill their treasuries." – NASB

Do not let your times of waiting be a time of frustration. You may be experiencing a traffic jam right now. My suggestion to you is to start praying or singing praises. It may not make the cars move any faster, but it is hard to remain in a state of frustration or be anxious when you are in the presence of the Lord. When life throws you a curve ball, hit it anyway and score a home run. You don't have to be super spiritual to give God the glory that He is due. He created everything. He deserves praise just for who He is.

Sometimes what we are waiting on is the feeling that God is there. There are times that we will walk into a wilderness, and there is seemingly nothing there but us and emptiness. After experiencing the feeling of God's presence, there is an expectation of miracles and an assurance that is very comforting. There will be times in our lives that we will not have that "feeling", and we must rest in what we know instead of what we feel. It is a time that builds faith although when it happens we may not agree that is what's happening.

Too many times we look for God only in the church where life changing miracles have happened, but there is also another side of God's presence. It's a very intimate presence that you can miss all too easily. You must be very quiet and still in order to experience it. I had a recent experience during a time when I felt very much alone, and God met my need in a very real and tender way.

My husband became ill unexpectedly and had to remain in the hospital. At this particular time, I didn't have the support of my family because they were all in another state. I had to take care of our two children by myself, keep my job, and still be there for my husband. That first night that he was there it was late, and I hadn't had the opportunity to call anyone from my church, my friends, or my family to alert them of the situation. I felt very much alone and yearned for someone that I knew and loved to hug me. Just a hug to reassure me that everything was going to be all right. Realizing that I was an adult I would simply have to tough it out and endure this time, but that was not satisfactory to God.

You see when I arrived home that night I hadn't been inside the house more than ten minutes when I heard a knock on the door. I became alarmed because I live out in the country and a knock on the door is not normal, especially at night. My first thought was that a stranger was there to harm my children and I. When I peered out the window I saw a very dear family friend. This woman had known my parents since long before I was even born, and I affectionately refer to her as mom number two. She had come over because she had grown concerned over her inability to contact me over the past few days. You must understand that both of our lives are so busy, we don't make a habit of calling one another on a regular basis. She told me that she had a strong urge to come over to see if there was anything wrong.

She was in amazement when I told her what had happened to my husband, and she reached over and gave me that hug that I had been yearning for all night. I knew at that moment that I wasn't alone in heaven or on earth, and that God would meet even the smallest of needs even when I felt He was the farthest from me. God is not just a mighty, powerful being. He is also a tender, loving, and caring Father. Spending time reading the word and praying will allow you to get to know all of His many aspects. He yearns to be with you, just as I yearned for that hug. There is a sweet blessing in spending that one on one time with God. It is a blessing that you can find nowhere else.

John 15:4-11
"Abide in Me, and I in you. As the branch cannot bear fruit of itself, unless it abides in the vine, so neither can you, unless you abide in Me. I am the vine, you are the branches; he who abides in Me and I in him, he bears much fruit; for apart from Me you can do nothing. If anyone does not abide in Me, he is thrown away as a branch, and dries up; and they gather them, and cast them into the fire, and they are burned. If you abide in Me, and My words abide in you, ask whatever you wish, and it shall be done for you. By this is My Father glorified, that you bear much fruit, and so prove to be My disciples. Just as the Father has loved Me, I have also loved you; abide in My love. If you keep My commandments, you will abide in My love; just as I have kept My Father's commandments, and abide in His love. These things I have spoken to you, that My joy may be in you, and that your joy may be made full." –
NASB

It is a great comfort to me to know that the Lord is always there, even when I feel the most alone. I have His promise that as long as I seek Him and endeavor to do His will, He will never leave me. As His children, we all have this promise as found in the below scripture.

Romans 8:38-39
For I am persuaded that neither death nor life, nor angels nor principalities nor powers, nor things present nor things to come, nor height nor depth, nor any other created thing, shall be able to separate us from the love of God that is in Christ Jesus our Lord. – NKJV

How often do we think God isn't there or doesn't care, and we go wandering off on a path by ourselves? How often do we receive direction from the Holy Spirit, and still turn aside to follow our own way because it looks different than we imagined? You would think that we would have learned by now that God knows what He is doing and that he loves us so powerfully that there is nowhere we can go to hide or be separated from it. If God says go, then we should trust him and go stepping out in faith. If He says stay, then we should stay. It may look like a dead end from our perspective, but then He can make a way where there was no way. He can provide in ways we never saw coming.

It's important, however, to know that God will not force himself upon you. He is not a brute. He is a loving father that understands who and what we are because he made us. He imparted gifts, talents, and abilities and takes delight in watching you discover them and walk in right relationship with him. He understands that you will from time to time do dumb and say stupid. He understands that you might shy away from an opportunity to grow your faith, but His love is poured out upon you anyway. Nothing you do or have done will shock him because he already knows and yet he still loves you, has plans for you, and looks forward to the day that you, too, embrace his plan for your life.

Isaiah 30:21
And your ears will hear a word behind you, "this is the way, walk in it," whenever you turn to the right or to the left. – NASB

Having a daily time of prayer along with the study of His word will keep you sensitive to the Holy Spirit's urging. Remember that our God is a God without boundary. He can go beyond our abilities, vision, and faith. He is the Alpha and the Omega. Your life aligned in obedience to the word of God will not give you an ordinary life, but an extraordinary one full of purpose, fulfillment, love, and blessing. Even if you are in a season of waiting, seek his will so you will know what you should be doing. Maybe it's a season of rest so you will be strong for a coming test, purpose, or calling. Regardless, follow after the Lord and the way will become clear.

John 14:6

Jesus said to him, "I am the way, and the truth, and the life; no one comes to the Father, but through Me." – NASB

Glenda C. Finkelstein

<u>Chapter Seven</u>

Stress Giant Defeated!

Our days are full of more things to do than hours in the day to complete them. We, therefore, rush to and fro not fully devoted to any of them. Quite frankly, the mouse on the wheel is getting more accomplished than we are. Sometimes we get ourselves into these messes, and sometimes the messes catch us. Regardless of who has whose tail we are too often the back seat driver. In addition, the driver is usually chaos and not the Holy Spirit.

Sometimes I feel as if I am the world's leading authority on stress and have developed it into an art form. I'm a wife, step-mother of two, mother of two, a writer, hold down a full time job, involved in my church, and try to maintain my sanity in the midst of it all. There are days that I feel as if I'm on a balance beam with a tray full of very fragile, expensive objects. It seems that many of them are falling off, but to catch the ones that are falling I must drop the ones that are still on my tray. It's a vicious cycle.

Glenda C. Finkelstein

This precarious situation reminded me of an experience in my youth when my parents took me to an amusement park. It was a fun and exciting day. I was about ten years old at the time, but I don't think I will ever forget this one particular ride. My father and I entered the car. The car we got into had a steering wheel. I immediately asked my father if I could drive. He said of course. I never felt so proud and confident in my entire life as I gripped that steering wheel knowing I could handle this. I was at the time too naive to know that the car we were in was on a track and that no turn of the wheel would alter its course. In the beginning, things were going along smoothly. I had a smile on my face knowing that I was in control of this vehicle. Then the unexpected happened. The car began going through walls. Its design was to do that, but I didn't want to go so I grabbed the wheel tightly and started turning it in hopes of avoiding a collision. All of my strength went into trying to regain control of this wild vehicle. Finally, with snow white knuckles and panting feverishly, I begged my father to take the wheel. That's when he leaned over and told me that the car was on a track and would go where the designers intended it to go and that no one needed to steer it. We laugh about it now, but that day I learned that we are not always in control even when we believe we are.

Not being in control of everything that affects your life can cause worry and strife. We are very selfish creatures declaring to the world that we got it all under control when in fact we are mice

76

running on the wheel. At least the mice know when to jump off, but not us humans. Oh no, we are going to stay on that wheel until we collapse just as I did on that ride. It wasn't until my strength had left me that I was ready to relinquish control.

Stress is one of those problems that has no physical substance, but can damage us just the same. We try to ignore it believing that because we can't touch it, see it, or taste it that doesn't exist, but it does. Christ also had to deal with it in the lives that He touched.

Luke 10: 38-42
Now as they were traveling along, He entered a certain village; and a woman named Martha welcomed Him into her home. And she had a sister called Mary, who moreover was listening to the Lord's word, seated at His feet. But Martha was distracted with all her preparations, and she came up to Him and said, "Lord, do You not care that my sister has left me to do all the serving alone? Then tell her to help me." But the Lord answered and said to her, "Martha, Martha, you are worried and bothered about so many things; but only a few things are necessary, really only one, for Mary has chosen the good part, which shall not be taken away. – NASB

Martha, like so many of us, gets so caught up in the hustle and the bustle that we lose sight of what's important. Instead of trying to balance too many things on our tray, we should put the whole tray down and sit at the Master's feet praying and reading the word. You protest that there are many important things on that tray and you can't possibly release them. I'm sure there are, but none are more important than time with the Lord. I'm not saying to neglect your responsibilities because everything has its place. I am saying that time with the Lord will help you prioritize and clean out the clutter of your life.

Luke 12:29-31
And do not seek what you shall eat, and what you shall drink, and do not keep worrying. For all these things the nations of the world eagerly seek; but your Father knows that you need these things. But seek first His kingdom and these things shall be added to you. – NASB

Doctors today are discovering that the root cause of many of our health problems is stress. There are countless ways man has devised to alleviate this condition. The world has employed everything from Aroma Therapy to Yoga to reduce our stress levels, but where does stress come from? I'm sure that if you asked any group of people you would get several answers. All of which would be correct such as too many things to do and not enough time to complete them. Harmony is not the current description of your home life. Your job makes you unhappy. You need a vacation from yourself. You worry about all the things that you cannot change. There are too many priceless objects falling off your tray and you can't get them all, and what is worse you can't stop to clean up the mess. To sum it up in a word, "Worry." The following question which Christ posed to his disciples is one

of the most common afflictions of man, who seems equally
helpless to conquer it on his own.

Matthew 6:27
And which of you by worrying can add a single cubit to his
life's span? – NASB

Worrying probably subtracts from our life's span. If you
have a problem with worrying, you probably have a Stress Giant in
your life. There is a power that can defeat this foe. You don't
have to be a warrior to fight and win. You just have to let go of
certain things and let God fight the fights you can't. David
couldn't even lift the sword that King Saul gave him to slay
Goliath. He won the fight with the tools of a shepherd, and a faith
in a God that was bigger than the giant he faced. We spend so
much time fretting over what we can't do, and worrying about
what we can't control that it leaves us helpless in dealing with
those things that we can fix.

1 Samuel 17:45-47
Then David said to the Philistine, "You come to me with a
sword, a spear, and a javelin, but I come to you in the name of
the Lord of hosts, the God of the armies of Israel, whom you
have taunted. This day the Lord will deliver you up into my
hands, and I will strike you down and remove your head from
you. And I will give the dead bodies of the army of the
Philistines this day to the birds of the sky and the wild beasts
of the earth, that all the earth may know that there is a God in
Israel, and that all this assembly may know that the Lord does

not deliver by the sword or by spear; <u>for the battle is the Lord's and He will give you into our hands</u>." -- NASB

I have struggled with worry for a good part of my life. Being <u>taught</u> that worry was just a part of being human I accepted it as being normal. My friends, nothing could be further from the truth. This is the one lie that has found an easy mark amongst all people, especially the church. One of the most valuable lessons I learned from my husband was that everything would work out in the wash, and it always does. Worry exists in the mind, and from the mind it stretches out to the rest of the body and poisons it. It causes headaches, stomach problems, depression, weakens the body's natural immunities, and the list continues. Worry accomplishes nothing for good and is the opposite of faith.

What about being concerned? Concern and worry are too very different things. Concern means that a situation warrants attention, correction, or any other actions that might bring about a solution to those circumstances. Worry means that this concern consumes you to the point that no good can come of it. There are situations that we can fix immediately, and others that will take a great deal of time. Whether it's quick or slow, we must always seek God's will in every situation and give Him <u>everything.</u> Even if you think you can handle it on your own, as I did on that ride when I was ten, give it to Him anyway because your control may be just a deception.

Jeremiah 17:7-8
Blessed is the man who trusts in the Lord and whose trust is the Lord. For he will be like a tree planted by the water, that extends its roots by a stream and will not fear when the heat comes; But its leaves will be green, and it will not be anxious in a year of drought nor cease to yield fruit. – NASB

This scripture doesn't promise that your life will be uneventful. It does, however, promise that by having faith in God the chaos around you will not touch you. You will remain strong and you will still prosper for His glory. How does one accomplish this? I am glad you asked that question.

Psalm 55:22
Cast your burden upon the Lord, and He will sustain you; He will never allow the righteous to be shaken. – NASB

I can hear the excuses coming now about how little I understand your particular situation. How your husband is unemployed, the rent is due, your baby is sick, or your wife is an alcoholic. You may have received a bad report from your doctor. Your child is having a baby out of wedlock. Your boss is a tyrannical dictator that is just waiting for an excuse to fire you. I could go on and on, but I am sure that you have already found your place or added it to the list. I don't mean to be disrespectful, but none of the needs listed above or added by you are bigger than our God. We serve the same God that delivered Israel from Egypt.

You say that Moses was special and saw a burning bush. God didn't deliver Moses only, but a nation.

Exodus 14:13-14,21-22,28
But Moses said to the people, "Do not fear! <u>Stand by</u> and see the salvation of the Lord which <u>He will accomplish for you today</u>; for the Egyptians whom you have seen today, you will never see them again forever. <u>The Lord will fight for you while you</u> <u>keep silent</u>. Then Moses stretched out his hand over the sea; <u>and the Lord swept the sea</u> <u>back by a strong east wind all night</u>, and turned the sea into dry land so the waters were divided. And the sons of Israel went through the midst of the sea on the dry land, and the waters were like a wall to them on their right hand and on their left. And the waters returned and covered the chariots and the horsemen, even Pharaoh's entire army that had gone into the sea after them; <u>not even one of them remained</u>. – NASB

I stand in awe of a God who in the midst of an impossible situation will make a miracle. Israel's deliverance was not by their hand or by Pharaohs. It was by the hand of God that both, His chosen people, and His enemies would acknowledge that day. If my God can take an entire nation through the middle of the Red Sea, holding it back until the Egyptians followed being destroyed by the same, surely my God can do anything. He can find my husband a job, provide your rent, deliver you from addictions, and heal your sick child. He will be with you and fight for you. He will comfort you in the valley of death. To overcome your stress, you must do only one simple thing. You must confess that He is God, who is ready and able to defeat the Stress Giant in your life.

Hebrews 12:1-2
Therefore, since we have so great a cloud of witnesses surrounding us, let us also lay aside every encumbrance, and the sin which so easily entangles us, and let us run with endurance the race that is set before us, fixing our eyes on Jesus, the author and perfecter of faith, who for the joy set before Him endured the cross, despising the shame, and has sat down at the right hand of the throne of God. – NASB

God has provided us many ways to defeat our giants. Besides casting our burden in fervent prayer before the throne of God, our first and most important step, He has given us each other in the corporate body of believers to share in both the burdens of life and the joys.

Galatians 6:2
Bear one another's burdens, and so fulfill the law of Christ. – NKJV

He has given us power through unified prayers.

Matthew 18:20
For where two or three are gathered together in My name, I am there in the midst of them. – NKJV

In order for the above two scriptures to be useful to us in times of trouble, we must first be honest with ourselves and with each other. There is a great misconception among believers that accepting Salvation will somehow make our lives perfect and that

Glenda C. Finkelstein

we should be happy all the time. We have taken the question, "How are you doing?" and lowered it to a standard greeting to which the expected response is, "I'm fine." As believers, we should never ask that question unless we are ready to bear a brother or a sister's burdens. Likewise when we answer, we should be honest. Pray together, but more than that become a doer of the word.

James 5:16
Therefore, confess your sins to one another, and pray for one another, so that you may be healed. The effective prayer of a righteous man can accomplish much. – NASB

Our needs come in all sizes and forms. The mature in faith need to be tenderhearted and forgiving, not judgmental so that James 5:16 is not just something we quote in Sunday School, but how we live. These needs may be spiritual, or physical like food, clothing, jobs, etc. There are many things that we can do to help. If you can't help them, ask the Holy Spirit to guide you to someone who can. Spiritual needs can be of greater distress than physical ones and need someone to stand in the gap for them as a prayer warrior. It is not a crime to express your need. Even our Savior needed ministering from time to time so he could receive strength enabling Him to minister to us.

Matthew 4:10-11
Then Jesus said to him, "Begone, Satan! For it is written, You shall worship the Lord your God, and serve Him only." Then the devil left Him; and behold, angels came and began to minister to Him. – NASB

Luke 22:41-43
And He withdrew from them about a stone's throw and knelt down and began to pray saying, "Father, if Thou art willing, remove this cup from Me; yet not My will, but Thine be done." Now an angel from heaven appeared to Him, strengthening Him. – NASB

If Christ, the Son of God, needed strengthening, how much more must we be there for each other so we can strengthen one another in His name. Maybe this time it's you who needs strengthening. Next time it maybe someone else, and because you received strength in a time of need, you are now able to help another. The tired can't run the race of endurance, only the well trained and rested can do that. The hungry will die. The thirsty will faint. The lonely will become bitter. We need to be the family that God designed us to be.

Above all remain faithful to the things of God. This Stress Giant may be a testing of your faith which by enduring it will make you stronger and bring you into a time of refreshing. These are the times to stay in the Word, pray more, worship more, and give more of yourself than you have ever given before. Remain obedient in your devotions, tithing, and worship. Don't let the cares and worries of this world choke out the priceless seed of

85

Glenda C. Finkelstein

hope and promise that Christ gave you upon accepting Him as your
personal Savior.

Matthew 13:22
And the one on whom seed was sown among the thorns, this is
the man who hears the word, and the worry of the world, and
the deceitfulness of riches choke the word, and it becomes
unfruitful." -- NASB

As I have written these chapters, the Lord has taught me by
the experience each and every lesson. This has been one of the
most difficult for me, but the most rewarding as well. During the
writing of this chapter, I went through a time of testing concerning
an issue that I have dealt with ever since the birth of my daughter.
My daughter was born severely ADHD, and anyone who has a
child like mine will immediately relate. Those of you who don't
can still relate to this story as it is relevant to obedience in a time
of trouble.

When you have a hyperactive child, you have stress in
every aspect and crevice of your life. Sixty seconds of silence and
peace is an eternity of rest and pleasure. Things were especially
bad at this particular time. It seemed to me that I would never get
the answer to my heart's prayer that my daughter would be able to
bring joy, not only to others, but to herself as well. To add to the
difficulties, I was sick in body as well as tired. It was a
Wednesday night in which we usually attend church services, but I
felt so badly I decided to stay home. Fortunately, the Holy Spirit

had other ideas. I felt this yearning on my face at the altars. Nothing I did relieved that tug on my spirit, and so I went reluctantly to a church that night. At least my spirit would leave me alone.

When I arrived at the church, I remember hoping that praise and worship wouldn't stop because my mind was so numb I didn't think I could absorb a sermon. I soon discovered that sitting in my seat in the sanctuary was still not giving my spirit what it desired. All I wanted was to be on my face at the altar. What I needed aspirin, decongestants, and vacations could never deliver. Much to my surprise and relief, the Pastor made an altar call at the beginning of service. I jumped out of my seat and went forward. The Pastor prayed for each person that went forward and under the anointing of the Holy Spirit gave each one of us a specific word from God. My word was, "No more." After uttering those two little words, I knew in my spirit that the light came on at the end of the tunnel. I had waited eight years to hear those two little words.

I received prayer that night not only from our Pastor but from godly women in the church. I left that service a very different person than the one who entered. My hope was restored, and my strength renewed knowing that the Lord had heard my cries. When I was at the last frayed end of my rope, God reached out and set my feet back on solid ground. Endurance was birthed in me that night. The days that followed were a time of testing, but I was very stubborn and hung on to that word with all my

Glenda C. Finkelstein

strength. I was not going to let the enemy steel what God had given me.

Psalm 46:1
God is our refuge and strength, A very present help in trouble – NKJV

The above was originally written in 1998, as I'm preparing this for a second edition release I'm profoundly reminded of all that we went through regarding my daughter. Now in 2014, so many years later in which there were many trials and struggles, I and my daughter have this testimony that she has grown up to be a beautiful woman of God. She graduated high school, developed those strengths that come on the positive side of ADHD, and her faith in God is unmovable. This year she'll be celebrating her second wedding anniversary to our beloved son-in-law, a former United States Marine, who has served honorably in both Iraq and Afghanistan. She has become my greatest joy and I'm extremely humbled and thankful that the Lord saw us all through the difficult times so that we can rejoice in these wonderful ones. God was and is faithful to give even this mother, the desires of her heart.

__Chapter Eight__

To sin, or not to sin?

That is the question and the decision that all of us must make each day. It doesn't matter how young or old you are or what station you hold, the temptation to sin is present. When people speak of sin, most immediately jump to the big ones like murder, stealing, and drug addiction. Although they are quite large to us, they didn't start out that way. They all began with very small compromises. Something that most people would not notice right away, but over time will lead to destruction. Society has even gone to the extremes of making excuses for these big sins sighting a bad upbringing. Although how you grow up contributes, everyone will eventually be able to make a choice to do what is right or what is wrong. You can choose to continue in a bad lifestyle, or change it.

Romans 8:6-8
For the mind set on the flesh is death, but the mind set on the Spirit is life and peace, because the mind set on the flesh is hostile toward God; for it does not subject itself to the law of

Glenda C. Finkelstein

God, for it is not even able to do so; and those who are in the flesh cannot please God. – NASB

Change is a very difficult thing. Perhaps it's because we have grown accustomed to the response that certain behaviors have brought. To change those behaviors will bring us into a realm called the unknown. After experiencing salvation, which is the point where God met you, now you must now meet Him. Yes, we have come to the point where we must understand the rules or what many have called the Do's and Don'ts of the Christian life. Many unwisely consider these things God's way of taking the fun out of life. Quite the contrary joy, life, and happiness are at the very heart of God and one we will explore in the next chapter.

To put it plainly, God has set down some rules on how a righteous life should be lived. Most of these rules are for our own protection, just as the rules of safety we have developed for our own children are there to protect them and not to deprive them of fun. A good example of a rule that every parent, who is worth anything, will have established is the rule, "Don't play with matches." Because matches, when used correctly by a responsible individual, are a useful tool, but when used by someone who is young and does not understand the consequences of a fire can become injured or die.

You can apply this analogy to any sin, but we will use sexual relations apart from the bonds of marriage as our comparison of sin verses God's law. Let's compare the results of the world's view of sexual relations to the way God intended it to be. The world's view says do it if it feels good with whomever you happen to be with. The world's results are a disease, unwanted pregnancy, abortion, broken trusts, and in many case's deaths because not all the diseases you come into contact with have a cure. By adhering to God's law and waiting until we marry and keeping that marriage undefiled will have the following results; intimacy, children, and joy. The world's way brings death, but God's way brings blessing and long life.

Romans 6:23
For the wages of sin is death, but the free gift of God is eternal life in Christ Jesus our Lord. – NASB

We could go through every possible sin verses' obedience to God's law and the result would be the same. Yet we don't have to sin. As I mentioned above, it's a choice that no one can make for you, nor can the devil make you do it. It's just a choice that you have to make when faced with situations that are contrary to God's law. How does one know what pleases God? Read the Bible. If you return to Exodus and read a few pages past the main Ten Commandments, you'll see a list of guidelines for the Hebrews to live by. I can hear some of you grumbling already, "Here come all the don'ts." Relax, you can sum them all up into treating each other with love, fairness, and respect. God isn't

Glenda C. Finkelstein

asking you to stand on your head and drink a glass of water while singing the Star Spangled Banner.

Perhaps we should pause for just a moment and define what sin is. In its simplest definition, it's anything that violates the original design. It's not just the breaking of a law it can be the presence of un-forgiveness for an offense. In fact, it's not always the in your face things that really cause the problems it's the hidden things that we hang on to that will do us in.

I can hear some of you saying that there are situations and temptations that are not so easy to walk away from, and you would be right. Some of them, we seemed to have slipped into all too easily, and at first it may not have started out as a sin. Then, little by little, come the small compromises. Don't act so spiritual, anytime you have to rationalize an action in your own mind you know you are on quicksand. Yet, there is no temptation that will come into your path that is new to this planet. Every man, woman, and child before you have dealt with these things long before you came along and will remain long after you have gone.

I Corinthians 10:13
No temptation has overtaken you but such as is common to man; and God is faithful, who will not allow you to be tempted beyond what you are able, but with the temptation will provide the way of escape also, that you may be able to endure it. – NASB

92

We now know that there is a way of escape in every situation, so remaining there to participate in the sin is your choice. Next time you are faced with temptation, remember that if God is providing a way of escape, He has a front row seat to your actions and nothing you do is secret before Him.

James 1:13-18
Let no one say when he is tempted, "I am being tempted by God." for God cannot be tempted by evil, and He Himself does not tempt anyone. But each one is tempted when he is carried away and enticed by his own lust. Then when lust has conceived, it gives birth to sin; and when sin is accomplished it brings forth death. Do not be deceived, my beloved brethren. Every good thing bestowed and every perfect gift is from above, coming down from the Father of lights, with whom there is no variation, or shifting shadow. In the exercise of His will He brought us forth by the word of truth, so that we might be, as it were, the first fruits among His creatures. – NASB

Let us look at making the good choice, now that we have a clear understanding of what sin is and its results. I would like to take it one step further than just making the good choice and move into not being tempted. Stay with me, any believer who has grown in Christ Jesus will testify that what once had them bound no longer holds them through the strength that Christ has given them. I'm not saying we will never experience temptation, I'm simply saying that by continuing to grow in the Lord you will move farther and farther away from sin and closer to God. It is part of partaking in the divine nature of God. The more you know God, the easier it is to discern what is not from Him.

Hebrews 5:13-14
For everyone who partakes only of milk is not accustomed to the word of righteousness, for he is a babe. But solid food is for the mature, who because of practice have their senses trained to discern good and evil. – NASB

A good illustration is that there are two coasts separated by a great sea. On one coast is sin and flesh, the opposite coast is God's holiness, and the great sea in the middle represents the separation of God from Sin. Salvation is dingy. A dingy is a one man boat equipped only with a set of oars. There is no room for supplies or excess baggage from your past life of sin. Salvation itself only gets you into the dingy, but you are still on the shore of sin. In order to grow in God, you must have faith, a trust that God will provide your every need.

As with most new believers, you quickly pull up anchor and start rowing for the opposite shore. When everything you know starts becoming small, you become nervous and head back to the shore you came from. The reason for your panic is that you still can't see God's shore from your vantage point. You realize that you forgot to bring food, water, clothes, etc. With great skill, you pack them into the dingy, cover them with a tarp so they don't get wet, and again you push off from shore. Unfortunately, you can't even make it past the sand bar because you sink not even six feet from shore. Your dingy is too heavy. In order to save yourself from sinking you toss the clothes, the cans of vegetables, but you save the corn chips. They are very light.

Now that you are afloat again, you start rowing. You decide to rest and let the current take you, but by the next morning you are right back where you started. How are you ever going to make it to the opposite shore? In frustration, you start looking around the boat and discover the word is in the boat. You begin to read it. You push off from shore again, but this time when it's time to rest you lay anchor so you don't drift back to shore.

The next day brings about a storm coming directly at you. You feel a breeze, which feels great at first, but then you hear the rumblings of thunder. You see the huge storm clouds coming at you with lightning flashing across the sky. You panic thinking that God left you out there to die, but He didn't. If you had only paid attention to where the gentle breeze was sending you, you would know what to do. Instead, you try to head back to shore. What you failed to realize was that the breeze was taking you to the Island of Prayer, a safe harbor from storms. Luckily another dingy finds you and tosses you a line pulling you to the Island of Prayer, but you have already taken quite a beating from the storm.

You decide to stay on this Island even though it is not your true destination. Your corn chips run out, so you must leave the harbor. Yet you have added to yourself the strength of prayer. You are now again out on the open water rowing towards your destination. You still can't see it, but you keep going. You have grown tired and hungry, but instead of rowing back to your shore you read the word and pray. Soon you see a school of fish leaping out of the water and into your boat. You have food! Then a small shower comes and fills you with fresh water.

Now that you are stronger, you do not fear the next storm you see and recognize the breeze in front of it. This time you discover the Island of Endurance. You find encouragement there among other believers. With hope and expectation, you go out again the next day. Before long the things of this world no longer shine as they once did. Now you are beginning to see the reflection of the glory and you continue to move towards it. You can still hear the noise from the shore you came from, but it is no longer clear or strong. Now because you have grown, you can hear the praise of Heaven even in the crashing waves of a storm.

Why then should we strive not to sin? It's not simply a matter of our well being or protection. It's not simply a matter of not testing God and His infinite patience. It's not even simply a decision between right and wrong? It's the very essence of what we became when we accepted Christ as our personal Savior.

2 Corinthians 6:16-18, 7:1
And what agreement has the temple of God with idols? For you are the temple of the living God. As God has said: "I will dwell in them and walk among them. I will be their God and they shall be My people." Therefore, "Come out from among them and be separate, says the Lord. Do not touch what is

unclean, and I will receive you. I will be a Father to you, and you shall be My sons and daughters, Says the Lord Almighty." Therefore, having these promises, beloved, let us cleanse ourselves from all filthiness of the flesh and spirit, perfecting holiness in the fear of God. – NKJV

Glenda C. Finkelstein

<u>Chapter Nine</u>

Be Happy!

We so easily forget our reward in dealing with the day to day struggles of our lives. You know what I mean the laundry, washing dishes, going to work, going to school, etc. This reward, however, is not just for when we get to Heaven. It belongs in the here and now. God concerns Himself with our happiness many times throughout the scriptures.

Philippians 2:1-4
If therefore there is any encouragement in Christ, if there is any consolation of love, if there is any fellowship of the Spirit, if any affection and compassion, make my joy complete by being of the same mind, maintaining the same love, united in spirit, intent on one purpose. Do nothing from selfishness or empty conceit, but with humility of mind let each of you regard one another as more important than himself; do not merely look out for your own personal interests, but also for the interests of others. – NASB

How wonderful and happy this world would be if everyone lived by this scripture. Think about it for a moment. To have the

Glenda C. Finkelstein

same mind and love as Christ, who gave us all, considering us more important than Himself, what a paradise? You say I must be living in fantasy land, no just Heaven.

Jeremiah 29:11
For I know the plans that I have for you declares the Lord, plans for welfare and not for calamity to give you a future and a hope. – NASB

Many people don't realize that Jeremiah 29:11 which is quoted so often was given to the people of Israel while they were in captivity in Babylon. This is a promise that no matter the circumstances you find yourself in, God still has a future for you.

Since the Word of God is faithful and true, why then do we have such difficulty finding happiness? Perhaps it's because we allow ourselves to fall into the world's view of happiness. The world declares loudly that you will find happiness in possessions, friends, family, etc. The truth is that even if we had nothing but the salvation of the Lord, we would have an eternal spring of happiness. Heaven, however, is not the only place where God dwells. So it is possible to tap into this happiness before we get there.

John 15:9-11
Just as the Father has loved Me, I have also loved you; abide in My love. If you keep My commandments, you will abide in My love; just as I have kept My Father's commandments, and abide in His love. These things I have spoken to you, that My

**joy may be in you, and that your joy may be made full. –
NASB**

There is no mention of waiting until we get to Heaven to
partake in this joy. Christ is speaking of right here and now, but it
will cost us one thing, obedience to Christ's commandments. I can
see the concern cross over your face. Nothing is free save
salvation, but there are only two commandments. Are not there
eight more?! Read, and see.

Mark 12:29-31
**Jesus answered, "The foremost is, Hear, O Israel! The Lord
our God is one Lord; and you shall love the Lord your God
with all your heart, and with all your soul, and with all your
mind, and with all your strength." The second is this, 'You
shall love your neighbor as yourself.' There is no other
commandment greater than these." – NASB**

Sound's familiar doesn't it. In order to have true happiness,
all we have to do is love. This love can't be an ordinary love it
must be a perfect love. Let me put it another way. We can't just
love what is familiar and comforting to us as the world loves their
own. We must love even our enemies. Oh, I can hear the excuses
coming. How can showing love to our enemies bring us
happiness? First of all, you can't bring happiness. Secondly,
loving our enemies is a commandment from Christ. I can see I am
losing some of you. I thought I understood happiness myself until

I started writing this chapter, and like all the others the Holy Spirit has given me a new understanding.

The first misconception about happiness is that it is a reward for a goal achieved. I will be happy when I reach a particular level of wealth. I will be happy when I have a boyfriend. I will be happy when I get that promotion. I will be happy when I get my own car. I will be happy when I can have a child. The second misconception is that happiness is just for the good times. None of these things in and of themselves will bring you that fulfillment that we associate with happiness. Many of these things can bring you joy as well as frustration, but if you can't be happy without them you can't be happy with them. In many cases, it just adds to the difficulty of finding happiness. Happiness is more of a state of contentment and existence rather than a tangible reward for our successes. Happiness is the hope in times of darkness.

Proverbs 17:22
A joyful heart is good medicine, but a broken spirit dries up the bones. – NASB

This scripture doesn't say anything apart from ourselves giving us happiness, nor does it say that this happiness comes from man. It speaks of the heart and the spirit that is the dwelling place of God in a believer's life. Unfortunately we are not always in tune with the spirit, vainly seeking after what the world seeks. If we seek after God, He will impart to us His happiness.

Job 8:20-21
Lo, God will not reject a man of integrity, nor will He support the evildoers. He will yet fill your mouth with laughter, and your lips with shouting. – NASB

Bildad spoke these words to Job in the midst of his suffering. No mere mortal man has ever suffered so much, and yet remained faithful. Most of us would have given up on the first round. Everything Job held dear was gone, but his trust in God was what kept him going. God rewarded him beyond what he could have hoped for during this time. I wonder how many rewards and blessing we have lost because something didn't go our way, and we stopped trusting in our God. Christ, who raised the dead, could only heal where there was faith. Just because we face trials, it doesn't mean that God has stopped caring or listening.

James 1:2-4
Consider it all joy, my brethren, when you encounter various trials, knowing that the testing of your faith produces endurance. <u>And let endurance have its perfect result, that you may be perfect and complete, lacking in nothing</u>. – NASB

The testing of our faith produces the endurance to bring us to the point where we lack nothing. I would like for you to note that faith is not an emotion. You can't feel faith. It is your commitment to trust and obey God regardless of the

Glenda C. Finkelstein

circumstances. We all seem to think that when we go through a trial we should be able to feel faith. You can't feel faith. You can feel peace, but not faith. Doubt may tempt us during a trial, but we can bind doubt in Jesus name. Faith is like a rope, and all we have to do is hang on to it with all of our strength.

1 Peter 1:6-9
In this you greatly rejoice, even though now for a little while, if necessary, you have been distressed by various trials, that the proof of your faith, being more precious than gold which is perishable, even though tested by fire, may be found to result in praise and glory and honor at the revelation of Jesus Christ; and though you have not seen Him, you love Him, and though you do not see Him now, but believe in Him you greatly rejoice with joy inexpressible and full of glory, obtaining as the outcome of your faith the salvation of your souls. – NASB

If we have God's word that He will never leave us or forsake us nor let us be shaken, we should be able to stand any test. Please note it says testing is not abandoning. We should, therefore, stand firm in our knowledge of His hope. Even death can't overcome Him, or us through our faith in Him. We are here to profess an eternal hope in God. If not, then why bother professing anything? There will come a day for each of us that debates will end, choices will be complete, and our possessions worth only the dust from which they were made. This is the day that all will know in whom they have, or have not believed.

104

Hebrews 6:19-20
This hope we have as an anchor of the soul, a hope both sure and steadfast and one which enters within the veil, where Jesus has entered as a forerunner for us, having become a high priest forever according to the order of Melchizedek. – NASB

What is this hope? This hope is nothing less than the great I AM Himself. The trinity, God the Father, God the Son, and God the Holy Spirit. The same powerful Holy God that created the universe. From the power of His glory that shines brighter than the stars to the tender precise architecture of the smallest atom. He breathed life into man. He loved us so much that He became a part of us and not only lived, but died for us a fallen race. Through the power of His resurrection, He claimed the final victory over hell and the grave. He brought to us a life that we cannot comprehend, but by accepting His gift as a little child can live just the same.

Psalm 71:5-6
For Thou art my hope; O Lord God, Thou art my confidence from my youth. By Thee I have been sustained from my birth; Thou art He who took me from my mother's womb; My praise is continually of Thee. – NASB

There is nothing like being in the presence of God. Ask God to fill you with His Spirit. Accept the cross of Christ, and pray humbly before Him. Believe in Him. Love Him with all your strength, with all your heart, with all your soul, and with all your mind. Allow your heart to be so full of Him, that you will live as you have never lived before. It doesn't matter how long you have

105

Glenda C. Finkelstein

been saved or have gone to church. It's impossible for any of us to
have spiritually arrived in our relationship with an infinite,
omnipotent God.

John 7:38-39
**"He who believes in Me, as the Scripture said, "From his
innermost being shall flow rivers of living water." But this He
spoke of the Spirit, whom those who believed in Him were to
receive, for the Spirit was not yet given because Jesus was not
yet glorified. – NASB**
      We have access to this power because of Pentecost. That
experience is just as real for us today, as for those so long ago. It's
for all God's children. His good is not weak or meager. It is
strong and generous. We have come to believe that happiness is
something that you can pursue. Happiness can't be caught,
bought, or awarded. It is a river that overflows from a life that
belongs to Him and Him alone. You don't have to be perfect
simply humble and pure of the heart seeking Him on a daily basis.
The closer you get the deeper you swim, and at some point you
won't be the only one who notices. You will be a light in a dark
world that shines so brightly, you won't need to ask for an
opportunity to witness for the Lord because the world will be
flocking to you.

Titus 3:5-7
**He saved us, not on the basis of deeds which we have done in
righteousness, but according to His mercy, by the washing of
regeneration and renewing by the Holy Spirit, whom He
poured out upon us richly through Jesus Christ our Savior,**

106

that being justified by His grace we might be made heirs according to the hope of eternal life. – NASB

These words and scriptures that have come alive to me are not an ABC plan of obtaining happiness. Happiness is not the goal. A right relationship with God is the goal and the rest will fall into place. If you truly want happiness that will bring you a river that flows from the living temple of God, start seeking Him right now. Don't wait a single second because it's a journey that is not complete until you are standing at the foot of the throne of God. Until that day it will get better and better, but only if you put God back on the throne of your heart.

Romans 15:13
Now may the God of hope fill you with all joy and peace in believing, that you may abound in hope by the power of the Holy Spirit. – NASB

Glenda C. Finkelstein

Chapter Ten

Keep the Sabbath!

In order for us to survive the daily grind, we must renew ourselves every week. We call this day the Sabbath and whether you celebrate it on Saturday or Sunday, it's the day set aside for the worship of God.

Genesis 2:1-3
Thus the heavens and the earth were completed, and all their hosts. And by the seventh day God completed His work which He had done; and He rested on the seventh day from all His work which He had done. Then God blessed the seventh day and sanctified it, because in it He rested from all His work which God had created and made. – NASB

I am not here to discuss the merits of different religions because it is our relationship with God that supersedes our religious titles. Religion will not get us to heaven. We will reach Heaven only by our relationship with God forged through the blood of Jesus Christ. We all belong to one body, the body of Christ.

Glenda C. Finkelstein

1 Corinthians 12:4-6
Now there are varieties of gifts, but the same Spirit. And there are varieties of ministries, and the same Lord. And there are varieties of effects, but the same God who works all things in all people. – NASB

This kind of lays to rest the old argument that my religious denomination is the right one or we are better than you because. Just because we are different does not give us the right to think we are better than another. That is pride and an abomination to God. God is an infinite Spirit and will receive any style of worship so long as it is in spirit and in truth. Whether your service is contemporary or traditional is only a matter of personal taste or attributed to the gifts which God has given you. The Sabbath, however, should be a Holy day in which you give your best to God.

Isaiah 58:13-14
If because of the Sabbath, you turn your foot from doing your own pleasure on My holy day, and call the Sabbath a delight, the holy day of the Lord honorable, and shall honor it, desisting from your own ways, from seeking your own pleasure, and speaking your own word, then you will take delight in the Lord, and I will make you ride on the heights of the earth; And I will feed you with the heritage of Jacob your father, for the mouth of the Lord has spoken. –NASB

How does one honor the day of the Lord? Go to church. I know that some of you have become turned off from the organization known as the church, but that is no excuse. There are

110

many who hold fast to the church which Christ established. After all it is not a building or a social club, it is God's people coming together to serve, worship, learn, and establish a fellowship that is pleasing to God, not man. If you attend church for any other reason than to serve the Lord, then you need to examine yourself. The church comes together for the soul purpose of lifting high the name of the Lord, and by doing this we will bring souls into the kingdom of God and make disciples. We are there to wage war against the powers of darkness through prayer, fasting, tithing, service and worship. We will explore the importance of each one later in this chapter. It doesn't matter if you come together in someone's home, a tent, or a huge cathedral we are the church, the body of Christ. To put the term church in perspective read this next scripture.

1 Peter 2:9-10
But you are a chosen race, a royal priesthood, a holy nation, a people for God's own possession, that you may proclaim the excellency of Him who has called you out of darkness into His marvelous light; for you once were not a people, but now you are the people of God; you had not received mercy, but now you have received mercy. – NASB

Anyone who has come to the saving knowledge of Jesus Christ falls into the above category. I don't know about you, but that makes me feel very special. Imagine you and me a royal priest, citizens of a holy nation who belong to God. But are not our daily devotions enough? No, that is just getting us ready for

Glenda C. Finkelstein

the main course. We still need a pastor, who fears God that will give us the word of God for us. These messages that only make us feel good and never challenge us to live a holy life will condemn us to hell. I'm not saying that every sermon should be hell fire and brimstone, but the church today is in bad need of conviction in many areas. How can we lift high the cross of Calvary without first taking it upon ourselves? Save us Lord from hypocrites, and from ourselves who have become blind to the fact that we may be one of them. What then should a true church be?

I Corinthian 12:12-31
For even as the body is one and yet has many members, and all the members of the body, though they are many, are one body, so also is Christ. For by one Spirit we were all baptized into one body, whether Jews or Greeks, whether slaves or free, and we were all made to drink of one Spirit. For the body is not one member, but many. If the foot should say, "Because I am not a hand, I am not a part of the body," it is not for this reason any the less a part of the body. And if the ear should say, "Because I am not an eye, I am not a part of the body," it is not for this reason any the less a part of the body. If the whole body were an eye, where would the hearing be? If the whole were hearing, where would the sense of smell be? But now God has placed the members, each one of them, in the body, just as He desired. And if they were all one member, where would the body be? But now there are many members, but one body. And the eye cannot say to the hand, "I have no need of you" or again the head to the feet, "I have no need of you." On the contrary, it is much truer that the member of the body which seem to be weaker are necessary; and those members of the body, which we deem less honorable, on these we bestow more abundant honor, and our unseemly members come to have more abundant seemliness, whereas our seemly
112

members have no need of it. But God has so composed the body, giving more abundant honor to that member which lacked, that there should be no division in the body, but that the members should have the same care for one another. And if one member suffers, all the members suffer with it; if one member is honored, all the members rejoice with it. Now you are Christ's body and individually members of it. And God has appointed in the church, first apostles, second prophets, third teachers, then miracles, then gifts of healings, helps, administrations, various kinds of tongues. All are not apostles are they? All are not prophets, are they? All are not teachers, are they? All are not workers of miracles, are they? All do not have gifts of healings, do they? All do not speak with tongues, do they? All do not interpret, do they? But earnestly desire the greater gifts. And I show you a still more excellent way. – NASB

Take a moment and meditate on Paul's words. Our differences are not what should divide us, but rather unite us. The next time anyone asks you what religion you are? The proper response in light of this scripture should be I am a Christian, and I worship at (Your church). There is one other thing that we did not cover yet. A true church is full of many servants. Every member is a servant or should be. There is a place and a purpose for each one. If you do not know what yours is, ask God and He will show you. In the body of Christ, we must all share one thing. In this, there can be no debate and is more powerful and necessary than any gift. We must have love. Without it we labor and serve in vain.

Glenda C. Finkelstein

I Corinthians 13:4-7, 13
Love is patient, love is kind, and is not jealous; love does not
brag and is not arrogant, does not act unbecomingly; it does
not seek its own, is not provoked, does not take into account a
wrong suffered, does not rejoice in unrighteousness, but
rejoices with the truth; bears all things, believes all things,
hopes all things, endures all things. But now abide faith, hope,
love these three; but the greatest of these is love. –NASB

You might think that this is all well and good and remind
me that the church is a group of very human people. News flash
the only perfect people exist in Heaven. If you are on this side of
the dirt, then you're not perfect. Those that don't go to church
regularly consider those who do fanatics or take offense at the fact
that regular church goers haven't arrived at perfection. All that
stuff about coming to church every Sunday is just so your pastor
will look good at general council right? God doesn't mind, after
all, He is a busy deity. No, no, no, no, no! How can we be so
blind? God takes our commitment to His house very seriously.

Deuteronomy 6:13-18
"You shall fear only the Lord your God; and you shall worship
Him , and swear by His name. You shall not follow other gods,
any of the gods of the peoples who surround you, for the Lord
your God in the midst of you is a jealous God, otherwise the
anger of the Lord your God will be kindled against you, and
He will wipe you off the face of the earth. You shall not put the
Lord your God to the test, as you tested Him at Massah. You
should diligently keep the commandments of the Lord your
God, and His testimonies, and His statutes which He has
commanded you. And you shall do what is right and good in
the sight of the Lord, that it may be well with you and that you
114

may go in and possess the good land which the Lord swore to give to your fathers. –NASB

I don't know about you, but He has my full undivided attention. I know most of us are more comfortable with the loving, compassionate side of our God, but He is a God of balance and is Holy. He paid a high price for us, and does not take kindly to sharing what he gave so much for with anything less than Himself. He made the Sabbath for us.

Mark 2:27
And He said to them, "The Sabbath was made for man, and not man for the Sabbath." –NKJV

You have to think of this one a while. The Sabbath He established for a man to secure a time of rest and focus on the source of his life, God. Everything a man would need was in place before he took his first breath. Our design was specific and wonderful, not random or chaotic. Our physical body must have a certain amount of sleep, nutrition, and cleanliness for it to function properly. Our spirit man has needs which when not properly maintained will not only affect us spiritually, but physically. These needs can only be met through worship, prayer, fasting, tithing, and service within a body of fellow believers. We shall explore all five along with several scriptures that barely scratch the surface of the many ways we need to be obedient. This obedience,

Glenda C. Finkelstein

when done with joy, will bring more blessings than you can
contain. We will begin with worship.

WORSHIP

Psalm 2:11
Worship the Lord with reverence, and rejoice with trembling.
– NASB

Never take lightly your participation in worship. He is
worthy of your respect and your honor. Your loyalty and
faithfulness must be without question.

Psalm 29:2
Ascribe to the Lord the glory due to His name; Worship the
Lord in Holy array. – NASB

Give your very best to him. Although the outside is what
most people judge by in giving your best, God sees the inside.
Humble yourself in prayer confessing your transgressions. Ask
His forgiveness so that when you praise the Lord He will see a son
or daughter without spot or blemish because they have been
washed in the blood of the Lamb.

Psalm 100:2
Serve the Lord with gladness; Come before Him with joyful
singing. – NASB

Worship is not a dirge. It's a time of ushering in the
presence of God. This should be a joyous task. It's more than a

responsibility. It's firstly an honor, to usher in the presence of the King of Kings and the Lord of Lords, and secondly, it's necessary to maintain a healthy relationship with our God.

Colossians 3:16
Let the word of Christ richly dwell within you, with all wisdom teaching and admonishing one another with psalms and hymns and spiritual songs, singing with thankfulness in your hearts to God. – NASB

There is nothing like a happy song to lift your spirits. The act of worship allows you to partake in the joy of God's presence. Worship is what sets the stage for miracles. How many times has it been said in scripture that by our own measure it will be given us? If we lack anything, it should never be the worship of God.

SERVICE

Ephesians 4:11-16
And He gave some as apostles, and some as prophets, and some as evangelists, and some as pastors and teachers, <u>for the equipping of the saints for the work of service</u>, to the building up of the body of Christ; until we all attain to the unity of the faith, and of the knowledge of the Son of God, to a mature man, to the measure of the stature which belongs to the fullness of Christ. As a result, we are no longer to be children, tossed here and there by waves, and carried about by every wind of doctrine, by the trickery of men, by craftiness in deceitful scheming; but speaking the truth in love, we are to grow up in all aspects into Him, who is the head, even Christ, from whom the whole body, being fitted and held together by that which every joint supplies, <u>according to the proper</u>

Glenda C. Finkelstein

working of each individual part, causes growth of the body for the building up of itself in love. – NASB

Being a Christian is not a spectator sport. You can't have a true salvation experience without also experiencing a desire to serve. That is the essence of what Jesus was, a servant. He was God, and He became our servant. Can we, who were saved by His sacrifice, be nothing more than pew warmers? I don't care how big or how small your congregation is, there is a place of service which God has chosen for you. It may not be the service you would have chosen, but God's will is more perfect than your wants.

Hebrews 12:28-29
Therefore, since we receive a kingdom which cannot be shaken, let us show gratitude, by which we may offer to God an acceptable service with reverence and awe; for our God is a consuming fire. – NASB

Our service is our thank you note to God for what he has done in our life. It is that simple. There is nothing complicated with God. There are no fine lines. Everything is very plain, but you must accept it on faith that is alive with service.

Romans 12:1
**I urge you therefore, brethren, by the mercies of God, to
present your bodies a living and holy sacrifice, acceptable to
God, <u>which is your spiritual service of worship</u>. – NASB**

Yes, worship is a form of service to God. Everyone can do
at least that much. Once more it should be a natural thing for
anyone who truly loves the Lord. If you find worship a burden,
then maybe you need to have some heavy one on one prayer with
God.

PRAYER

Isaiah 56:7
**Even those I will bring to My holy mountain, and make them
joyful in My house of prayer. Their burnt offerings and their
sacrifices will be acceptable on My altar; <u>For My house will be
called a house of prayer for all the peoples</u>. – NASB**

The church is God's house of prayer. Why did God
establish His house as a place of prayer? I believe you will find
that there are many reasons for making prayers to God. One reason
for prayer that accompanies each prayer ever given is that it is a
time of intimacy with our Heavenly Father.

Luke 22:40
**When He came to the place, He said to them, "Pray that you
may not enter into temptation." – NKJV**

Glenda C. Finkelstein

Prayer gives us strength to overcome and resist sin. When you consider the evil days in which we live, we can't afford not to pray. It's our lifeline to living a holy life.

Matthew 21:22
And whatever things you ask in prayer, believing, you will receive. – NKJV

Prayer is a time to make your needs and desires known to God. This is not a blab and grab proposition where you come to God only when you need something. Prayer should be a precious time and should never be far from you.

I Thessalonians 5:17
Pray without ceasing. – NKJV

Many people refer to this scripture as meaning to stay in an attitude of prayer. When you think about it prayer is a time of humbleness, thankfulness, and acknowledging a dependency upon God. Dependency upon God is not a weakness, but a strength. When we acknowledge our dependency on God, it declares to the Lord that we are trusting in Him and not our flesh.

Colossians 4:2
Devote yourselves to prayer, keeping alert in it with an attitude of thanksgiving. – NASB

Praying consistently is what will bring about the will of God in your life. This is what will heal, deliver, and bring forth souls into the kingdom of God. God established prayer as a means of communicating with His children, and not only when we need something. How and why should we pray so often you ask? Good question and we just happen to have the answer.

James 5:13-16
Is anyone among you suffering? Let him pray. Is anyone cheerful? Let him sing praises. Is anyone among you sick? Let him call for the elders of the church and let them pray over him, anointing him with oil in the name of the Lord; and the prayer offered in faith will restore the one who is sick, and the Lord will raise him up, and if he has committed sins, they will be forgiven him. Therefore, confess your sins to one another, and pray for one another, so that you may be healed. The effective prayer of a righteous man can accomplish much. – NASB

Praying for those in the body of Christ is not our only responsibility for even sinners will take care of their own. What then makes us different from the world?

Matthew 5:44-48
"But I say to you love your enemies, and pray for those who persecute you in order that you may be sons of your Father who is in heaven; for He causes His sun to rise on the evil and the good, and sends rain on the righteous and the unrighteous. For if you love those who love you, what reward have you? Do not even the tax-gatherers do the same? And if you greet your brothers only, what do you do more than others? Do not even the Gentiles do the same? Therefore you are to be perfect, as your heavenly Father is perfect." – NASB

Glenda C. Finkelstein

We are to be perfect?! But we are sinners saved by grace! How can we be perfect?! Don't panic. We are to be perfected through prayer, fasting, worship, tithing, and service. Living our lives as if we were the dwelling place of God, will change the way we live. Will we make mistakes? Yes, but God will forgive us so long as we repent and go on in Him. Will we face trials? Yes, but we will be stronger because of it and gain a testimony that will overcome the enemy. Each day we will come closer to the mark than we did the day before. We can do all these things through Christ, and reach the goal established for us by God.

FASTING

Joel 2:12-13
"Yet even now," declares the Lord, return to Me with all your heart. And with fasting, weeping, and mourning; And rend your heart and not your garments." Now return to the Lord your God, for He is gracious and compassionate, Slow to anger, abounding in loving kindness, and relenting of evil. – NASB

Fasting is something that not many people do anymore. It's a time of crucifying our flesh to strengthen our spirit and is always accompanied by prayer. God knows you are really serious when you fast. It's the most effective means of seeking the Lord's will for the decisions you make. It can also be a tool for coming into a closer walk with Him. It's not done with a proud heart, but one of humility. It marks a true commitment in your life to our God.

Acts 13:2-3
<u>And while they were ministering to the Lord and fasting,</u> the Holy Spirit said, "Set apart for Me Barnabas and Saul for the work to which I have called them." Then when they had fasted and prayed and laid their hands on them, they sent them away. – NASB

Please note that they fasted twice. The first time was while they were ministering to the Lord, or a time of waiting for the Lord to show them His will. The second time they fasted was in response to the Lord's answer. The church at this time was very young and persecution was intense. Many faced death because they professed the gospel of Jesus Christ. By praying and fasting, they received power to do the work the Lord had set before them.

There are so many people who are looking and seeking something to fill a void within themselves. They look for it in relationships, jobs, education, and sometimes drugs and alcohol. Yet these things always leave you empty. A true relationship with God is the only thing that can fill those empty places. We see how the world around us suffers, and we do nothing. We call to God and ask Him to heal our land, but have we humbled ourselves? Are we too good to get our spiritual hands dirty? Do we have a burden for souls to where we will fast and pray rending our hearts for the lost?

TITHING

Leviticus 27:30
Thus all the tithe of the land, of the seed of the land or of the fruit of the tree, is the Lord's; it is holy to the Lord. – NASB

Giving back to the Lord is one of the biggest stumbling blocks humans have, but it plainly states that it already belongs to God. We should, therefore, return it to our Lord in faith and joy knowing that the Lord has a purpose for everything. I suspect that if everyone gave their tithe that no one would go to bed hungry, naked, or would lack for any good thing. Yet we cling to our check books like a life raft. In a time span of five years, my husband and I have faced unemployment. I have faced it once, and my husband twice. Trust me when I say that there is nothing in that check book that can save you from the unexpected storms of life. A tithe is God's, and not yours.

Malachi 3:7-12
"From the days of your fathers you have turned aside from My statutes, and have not kept them. Return to Me, and I will return to you," says the Lord of hosts. "But you say, 'How shall we return?' "Will a man rob God? Yet you are robbing Me! But you say, <u>How have we robbed Thee? In tithes and offerings.</u> You are cursed with a curse, for you are robbing Me, the whole nation of you! <u>Bring the whole tithe into the storehouse, so that there may be food in My house, and test Me now in this,</u>" says the <u>Lord of hosts, "if I will not open for you</u> the windows of heaven, and pour out for you a blessing until it

overflows. Then I will rebuke the devourer for you, so that it may not destroy the fruits of the ground; nor will your vine in the field cast its grapes," says the Lord of hosts. And all the nations will call you blessed, for you shall be a delightful land," says the Lord of hosts.—NASB

This is a very stern reprimand by the Lord, and we see that there is a purpose for our tithes. Not giving our tithes will bring a curse. Some of you may not even recognize that you are under a curse, but how many jobs do you have to work to make ends meet? How much debt do you have? How much overtime do you need to work to pay the bills? By obeying the word of God, there is a blessing of provision to the point that you cannot contain it. I can see that some of you are squirming in your chairs. You have never tithed your ten percent. This probably more than anything else is a true act of faith. Take the leap. We did. We were in debt and had never incorporated tithes into our budget. I am not going to tell you that we did it overnight because we didn't. We prayed for wisdom in our finances, asked for forgiveness for our selfishness, and actively worked toward the goal of a tenth of our first fruits. Each time we took another step of faith, God met us. Every time a need arose, God provided. He promised that He would never leave nor forsake you. His word is faithful and true.

Glenda C. Finkelstein

2 Corinthians 9:7
Let each one do just as he has purposed in his heart; not grudgingly or under compulsion; for God loves a cheerful giver. – NASB

To truly love the Lord is to keep His commandments. He is our provider, our tower of refuge, our strength, and our trust. I would be amiss to declare that I have perfected everything stated here. I am, however, running the race to win. I may not have been perfect yesterday, but today is a new day in the Lord. I will take ground, and move on in Him. I pray that you too will do the same. These scriptures are only a glimpse of God's heart. Take His word and read it for yourselves. If we truly are desirous of a mighty move of God, nothing will speak louder to Him than our obedience.

Proverbs 29:18
Where there is no vision, the people are unrestrained. But happy is he who keeps the law. – NASB

<u>Chapter Eleven</u>

Now I lay me down to sleep...

You have made it safely through the day. Perhaps you picked up a few bumps and bruises and maybe you gave the term bad hair day a whole new meaning, but you are still breathing. If you are a woman, your pantyhose has probably bunched up at the ankle by now. Men have acquired that rugged five o'clock shadow look with some deformed thing that use to be a tie poking forth from their shirt. Your children have that orphaned look with a precisely placed smudge of dirt somewhere if not everywhere on their face.

Yes, the battle weary family has returned home to their refuge of safety away from the world. Everyone plops down onto their own soft, comfy spot in the house. They wait for supper to be ready, baths, and their favorite show to come on so they can relax and futilely pretend that the world will go away. Heavy sighs declare, "leave me alone," and is rarely honored because there are now dishes, homework, and laundry to do. Somewhere among the

Glenda C. Finkelstein

duties you yearn for a time of peace and serenity. A good night's sleep, when you can get one, just doesn't do it anymore. Morning comes way too quickly, and the weekend just isn't long enough. The worries of our day to day existence seem to smother any such feelings of renewal.

It will probably come as no surprise when I tell you that if we will only come back to the Lord's plan and design for our lives that even our sleep will rejuvenate us. It is amazing to me to discover that God has even designed how we should rest. If we apply these things, I believe we will tap into a paradise that no vacation could ever supply.

Jeremiah 31:25
For I satisfy the weary ones and refresh everyone who languishes. –NASB

How many nights have we laid awake languishing over troubles that were looming in the immediate future? Did we think to bring them to the Lord? We have missed so much contentment and joy because we try to put God in the Sunday only box instead of the, I need Thee every hour throne. When did we turn and walk our own road taking only a brief detour on Sunday for church? People, including myself, have had such wonderful experiences in church only to leave it there. We need to take these things with us. I have been striving more and more to bring home that "To Go" package from church home with me.

Proverbs 3:21-26
**My son, let them not depart from your sight; Keep sound
wisdom and discretion, So they will be life to your soul, and
adornment to your neck. Then you will walk in your way
securely, and your foot will not stumble. When you lie down,
you will not be afraid; When you lie down, your sleep will be
sweet. Do not be afraid of sudden fear, nor of the onslaught of
the wicked when it comes; For the Lord will be your
confidence, and will keep your foot from being caught. –NASB**

Keeping wisdom and discretion in every decision we make.
Living what we believe. Employing everything we have learned
about our God will deliver us from counting sheep and ulcers.
There will be no need to worry about the day's troubles or those
coming tomorrow because the Lord our God is all that we will ever
need. If you love Him, keep His commandments and He will keep
you.

Psalm 19:7-10
**The law of the Lord is perfect, restoring the soul; The
testimony of the Lord is sure, making wise the simple. The
precepts of the Lord are right rejoicing the heart; The
commandment of the Lord is pure, enlightening the eyes. The
fear of the Lord is clean, enduring forever; The judgments of
the Lord are true; they are righteous altogether. They are
more desirable than gold, yes, than much fine gold; Sweeter
also than honey and the drippings of the honeycomb. –NASB**

A life filled with joy, peace, and faith aren't a blessing
bestowed upon a select few, but is sought after daily by those who
really want it. You must seek it and desire it more than anything in

your life. You can't be half way there with God. I would like you to think about your life for a moment. Really examine it. You don't have to go too far to find a situation for this purpose. This past week will suffice rather nicely. Are there any moments that you feel were not your greatest? It does not have to be some humongous mistake like robbing a bank. It could be a judgmental thought, a wrong attitude, or being short and snippy with your child because they interrupted your concentration. Really any moment that would not be pleasing to God will qualify. We all have those moments that we really don't want anyone to know about, but God does. Yet many of us will continue acting as if we can hide these things from Him. Blaming someone else is not the answer either. Sometimes we simply have to swallow that bitter pill and admit we were wrong. This is very hard for me to do. I tend to be a bit of a perfectionist, and go out of my way not to make mistakes. Unfortunately, I am not perfect and discover all too quickly that I have not given God total reign in every aspect of my life. Don't go super spiritual on me. Everyone tries to hang on to that old person in some form or fashion. It's like the junk closet of your house.

This room is dirty and cluttered with all the guilt, shame, and pain of our deepest hurts and sins with walls of un-forgiveness and bitterness that we have allowed to grow untended. Yet in order to have the kind of life described in the above scriptures we must let God into that place. You say, No! God is holy! He will turn away from me when He sees just how wretched I really am. If God was going to turn away from you, Christ would have never gone to the cross. It's for this room of darkness in your life that hides behind your Sunday best that Christ came to heal. Spiritual surgery is not an easy thing, but once you remove the cancer life will be new, fresh, and clean. We cannot do this in our own strength, but only through the love and compassion of Jesus Christ.

Matthew 11:28-30
Come to Me, all who are weary and heavy-laden, and I will give you rest. Take My yoke upon you, and learn from Me, for I am gentle and humble in heart; and you shall find rest for your souls. For my yoke is easy, and My load is light. –NASB

Christ is not going to condemn you so why condemn yourselves to living with this burden of secretly buried sin. The closer we get to God, the more we realize that we can't take this stuff with us. We must cast it off, or become stagnate unable to move forward. God is full of mercy. No matter what has happened to you in your life, He is there for you. There is peace that you can possess that this world cannot touch, but you must go into the holy of holies to get it. Just as Israel had to take the land that God promised them. It was theirs, but they had to take it. As long as they kept their eyes firmly on God they were victorious, and just like us when they removed their eyes they stumbled.

Glenda C. Finkelstein

Joshua 1:13
Remember the word which Moses the servant of the Lord
commanded you, saying, The Lord your God gives you rest,
and will give you this land. –NASB

Nothing in this world can come to the gates of Heaven, but the wall of "Why," seems to overshadow your life. You may have a thousand questions that is blocking your way to the Father. Don't let yourselves be caught up in that. My children, when they were little, would ask, why? I would answer. Then they would ask why again, and again, and again. Finally, I just told them, "Because this is the way it is." Understanding is not necessarily a requirement, only acceptance, and obedience. Even the disciples of Christ had a difficult time understanding everything Christ told them, and they ate with him, walked with him, and heard his voice. God sees the entire picture from beginning to end from generation to generation of every single person whoever graced this planet and those who are yet to come. Trust in the Lord your God, and keep on seeking Him whether you have all the answers or not.

The more you seek, the more God will reveal. It doesn't matter if you are young or old. It doesn't matter that the things of this world are passing away. We have a hope that is eternal that breaks the bindings of our mortality. Nor do we have to be in heaven to enjoy that which our Heavenly Father has promised us. We can partake now, but we have to be willing to actively pursue a holy life.

2 Corinthians 4:15-18
For all things are for your sakes, that the grace which is
spreading to more and more people may cause the giving of
thanks to abound to the glory of God. Therefore we do not
lose heart, but though our outer man is decaying, yet our inner
man is being renewed day by day. For momentary, light
affliction is producing for us an eternal weight of glory far
beyond all comparison, while we look not at the things which
are seen, but at the things which are not seen; for the things
which are seen are temporal, but the things which are not seen
are eternal. – NASB

How we live our day to day life is our testimony. When the world sees us, do they see their own or do they see Christ? We have authority through Jesus Christ to overcome sin and live a victorious life. We are free to live our lives with no walls to hold us back. All we have to do is see that with God, there are no walls only life. Knowing that God is with us always all we have to do is learn, pray, serve, and especially love. What you believe and trust in will bring joy or strife in your life. What you live will bring abundant life or death. God is not a religion, but our creator and our life. Apart from Him we are nothing. We are His bride bought with a price. It is time we grow up and prepare ourselves for the wedding. When He comes, will He catch you sleeping or on the alert? And finally, how does one live this life of preparedness?

I Peter 4:10-11
As each one has received a special gift, employ it in serving one
another, as good stewards of the manifold grace of God.
Whoever speaks, let him speak, as it were, the utterances of

God; whoever serves, let him do so as by the strength which God supplies; so that in all things God may be glorified through Jesus Christ, to whom belongs the glory and dominion forever and ever. Amen. – NASB

www.ingramcontent.com/pod-product-compliance
Lightning Source LLC
Chambersburg PA
CBHW060308050426
42448CB00009B/1766